READER'S THEATER
for Real-Life Mysteries

Author
Christina Hill, M.A.

Editor
Sara Connolly

Editor in Chief
Brent L. Fox, M. Ed.

Creative Director
Sarah M. Fournier

Cover Artist
Diem Pascarella

Illustrator
Renée Mc Elwee

Imaging
Amanda R. Harter

Publisher
Mary D. Smith, M.S. Ed.

Teacher Created Resources
12621 Western Avenue
Garden Grove, CA 92841
www.teachercreated.com

ISBN: 978-1-4206-1700-9

©2022 Teacher Created Resources

Made in U.S.A.

For standards correlations, visit
http://www.teachercreated.com/standards/

Teacher Created Resources

Table of Contents

Introduction

What happened to the settlers who vanished from the Roanoke colony? Is there really a monster in Lake Champlain? And what was the mysterious substance that rained down over a small town in Washington? Real-life mysteries like these are a source of fascination for adults and children alike. These mysteries challenge our view of the world and can open our minds to new possibilities. In this book, real-life mysteries are presented in reader's theater format for an engaging activity that the whole class will love.

Research strongly indicates that reading text with fluency leads to student success in a variety of subject matters. Fluency is the ability to read a text with the appropriate speed, intonation, accuracy, and expression. Common Core literacy standards require students to "read grade-level text orally with accuracy, appropriate rate, and expression on successive readings." However, teachers and parents may struggle with finding ways to evaluate this level of fluency in their young readers. Simply reading and rereading to increase fluency may feel forced and may not provide students with the proper tools needed for reading comprehension. Additionally, not every young reader feels comfortable reading aloud. Shy students or struggling readers may dread oral reading or feel anxious standing on a stage. Memorizing lines can also be stressful and intimidating to younger students. So what is the solution? Cue *Reader's Theater for Real-Life Mysteries*!

Although repeated reading of a text is one of the best ways for students to master fluency, no one wants to read the same text over and over *unless* it is something truly engaging! Reader's theater gives young readers the opportunity to embrace both oral reading and repeated readings in an exciting and fun way. The plays in this book offer fictional retellings of dramatic real-life unsolved mysteries. The drama and mystery of the stories will hook the reader and the audience into exciting mysteries. Students will learn to work together as a team as they perfect their lines for the culminating project—performing the play for parents, other students, or even a recorded online stream.

You may be wondering why reader's theater is not performed often in the classroom. Some teachers worry that it will take up too much time or require too much work to present a successful performance. *Reader's Theater for Real-Life Mysteries* is designed to be simple and seamless. There are no props or costumes required. Each easy-to-follow lesson plan includes historical background content, vocabulary activities, and a culminating activity and journal page. Your student will be practicing reading fluently and building their reading comprehension skills all while having fun!

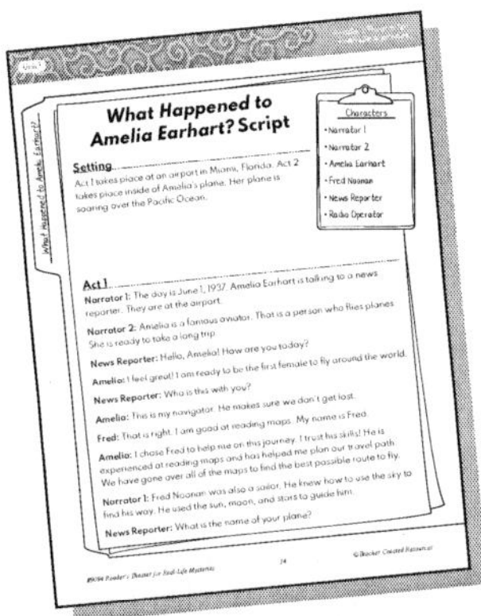
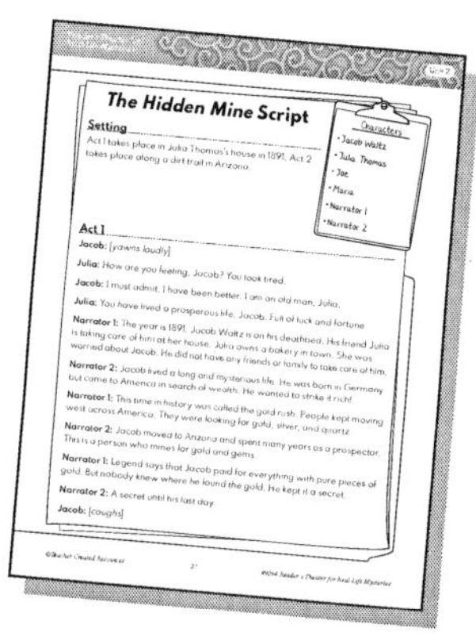
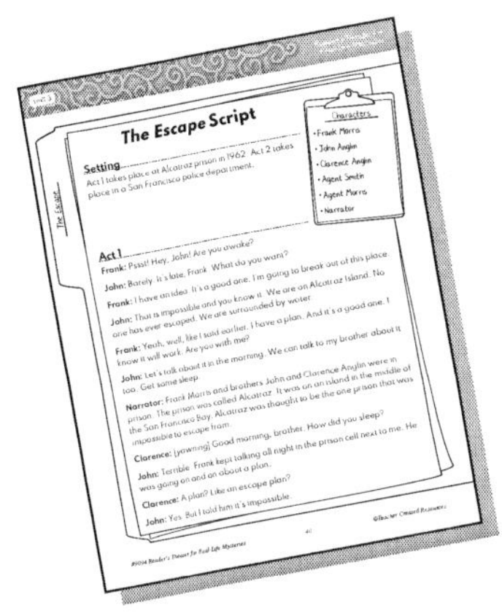

How to Use This Book

Reader's Theater for Real-Life Mysteries offers eight engaging scripts designed to be used with small groups of six students. Each play is divided into three higher-level reading parts and three lower-level reading parts. (This information is provided on the *Characters* page for each unit.) The roles in each script are listed from highest-reading level (high 3rd grade) to lowest (high 1st grade). Note that the *Characters* page is provided as a teacher-only page so that you can distribute the roles according to students' reading abilities. Although the roles are differentiated, students will not know which parts are harder than others. This gives everyone an equal chance to shine! If you have fewer than six students, you can offer a strong reader the chance to play two different roles at once. You can also consider performing the script more than once and having students play different roles each time!

Each lesson includes a short background description of the real-life mystery and some potential theories offered over time. Review this information before distributing the play and discuss the background information with students. Each play is a fictional retelling of a real-life event. While dialogue and creative liberties were taken in writing the play, most of the characters are based on real people, and—more importantly—the events actually did happen. All eight of the mysteries are still considered unsolved as of this writing.

Key vocabulary words are provided on the lesson plan pages. Consider frontloading the words with students before practicing the scripts to ensure they understand these higher-level content words.

The best part about reader's theater is the simplicity! No stage, props, or costumes are required. However, if students are passionate about providing these elements, feel free to let them run with it.

Badges that students can decorate are provided for each character. There are various ways to use these badges:

- Make headbands out of construction paper and staple the badges to the headbands for students to wear.
- Pin the badges to students' shirts.
- Tape the badges to rulers, and have students hold them up while reading.
- Tie the badges to yarn, and have students wear them as necklaces.
- If students will be sitting in chairs, tape the badges to the wall above their heads.

How to Use This Book *(cont.)*

Provide each student with at least one copy of the script. (**Note:** If preferred, an additional copy of the script can be given to each student so they can practice reading at home.) Tell students to highlight their parts of the script so they do not miss their lines. Then practice, practice, practice! Give students silent-reading time so they feel comfortable with their own parts before arranging them in small groups for oral-reading practice.

While an actual performance is not required, the culminating performance day is something that students may look forward to the most. Consider having small groups perform for the whole class, or invite other classes to watch. A performance day where parents are invited to be the audience may be fun for students and a great way to connect home and school learning. Be sure to record the performance and share the video with parents. Another option is to do the whole performance as a livestream online. See page 8 for more information on online performances.

Once students have mastered their parts with fluency, you can assess their reading comprehension. The activity sheet offers comprehension questions and provides students with a self-assessment rubric. Review the self-assessment rubric so that students understand how they will be scoring their performance. Students will benefit if they have the chance to listen to their own performance. See pages 7–8 for more information on recording performances.

After students have practiced and performed the reader's theater, you can conclude the unit with a writing activity. The final journal page provides students with the opportunity to express their own ideas and theories about what really happened during these mysterious moments in history!

Note: *The reader's theater plays in this book are fictional retellings of real-life events. They were drawn from published materials and interviews. For narrative purposes, the stories contain fictionalized scenes and dialogue. The views, opinions, and dialogue belong to the characters only and may not be true representations of the views, opinions, and dialogue held or spoken by the real-life individuals.*

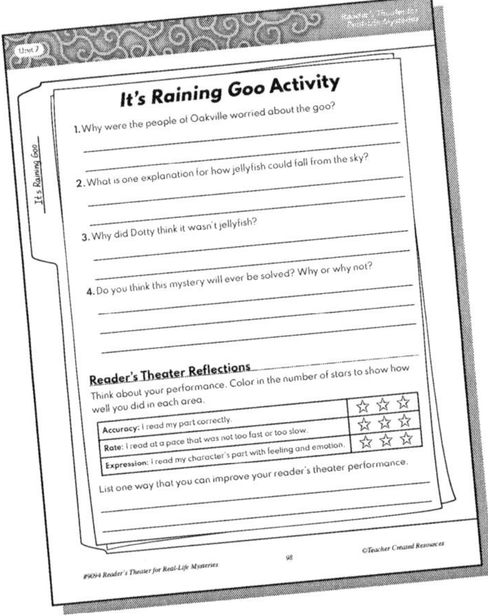

Hints for the Director

Take a deep breath. Being the director may seem intimidating for a theater production, but not for reader's theater! You will be pleasantly surprised at how little effort it takes to create a fun and engaging theater performance. Here are some tips to help you direct your readers into producing a successful performance:

- Carve out time whenever possible. It may seem daunting and impossible to fit a reader's theater play into an already tight classroom schedule. But it only takes is few minutes a day for students to practice reading their parts. If you find yourself wrapping up class ten minutes early one day, tell students to pull out their scripts. You can also have the scripts be part of a language arts center or silent-reading time.

- Reading for fluency is a Common Core standard. Instead of viewing the performance as an extra task, simply build it into your language arts block and feel confident that students are meeting that standard in a fun and engaging way.

- Reader's theater is a collaborative project. Not only will your students be learning to read with fluency, but they will also be learning to work together as a team. Encourage students to support one another in this process. Strong readers can serve as mentors or coaches to struggling readers and help guide them on their path to fluency.

- Remind students that the goal is *not* memorization! Reader's theater is about reading. The goal is to read their lines with expression, confidence, and accuracy. Students need to pay attention to punctuation and pause accordingly. They should speak in a voice that is loud enough so that everyone can hear them. They should use proper inflection and speed when reading their parts.

- Meet one-on-one with each student at least one time. Echo reading is a great way to teach fluency. Read the student's line out loud to them first, modeling correct inflection, intonation, speed, and expression. Then, have the student repeat the line back to you. This will also be an opportunity for you to assess whether each student knows how to read and understand each word in their part.

- Make sure students have access to their highlighted scripts at all times. Consider having students create construction-paper covers to protect their scripts. If you have extra plastic folders, you can punch holes in the scripts and keep them in folders for protection.

Hints for the Director *(cont.)*

- Review basic theater rules with your students. Remind them to be still and extra quiet when it is not their turn to read. This will ensure that each student's part is heard. If they stumble over a word or make a mistake, the show must go on! Tell students to relax and do their best.

- Have students follow along the entire time the play is being performed. Listening is an important part of a reader's theater performance. If they do not follow along, they will miss their turn!

- If you find that your readers are struggling with knowing when it is their turn to speak, assign a student to be the director's assistant. If there is a pause during the play and no one knows whose turn it is, the assistant will quietly nod or make eye contact with the person who should be reading.

- Self-assessment is an important part of understanding fluency. Have students record their parts using Flipgrid, Seesaw, or any other video-recording app your classroom uses. Then, have each student watch their own performance. Have them take notes for ways they can improve their own fluency. Did they mumble? Was there a line they stumbled over? Were they loud enough? Did they read too fast or too slow?

- Remember that no stage is required. Your production can be just a line of chairs at the front of the classroom or set in a small-group circle.

- If you invited parents to come to the classroom, students can create playbills for them. They can create a backdrop for their play or decorate the classroom in any way that fits the script. If you have multiple small groups performing different scripts, you can have each group create a banner with the title of the play to hang behind their group. Props are not needed. Remember that students will need to hold their scripts—this will limit the use of any props.

- Don't forget to tell students to have fun! This is their chance to give it their all and show off their reading and acting skills. Embrace the timeless quality of theater production, and break a leg!

Tips for Online Reader's Theater

Reader's theater is easily adaptable to distance learning groups using Zoom, Google Meet, Skype, or whichever videoconferencing software your school uses. If you are teaching a distance-learning group, provide each student with a copy of the script. They can highlight their parts either on a printed copy or an electronic one. You can follow the lesson plan the same way you would in the classroom. Provide students time to practice their lines individually. You can also schedule a one-on-one meeting with each student to listen to them read their individual parts with fluency and to ensure that they understand their lines. Then, assign breakout rooms of small groups in Zoom or Skype so students can practice the script together. Consider allowing students to change their Zoom names to match their roles in the play. Once students feel comfortable reading their parts with fluency, designate a final-performance day.

While distance or online learning presents challenges to some forms of instruction, it will not be a problem for reader's theater. In fact, you can work with teachers and students from anywhere in the world. Consider pairing up with another school to perform the play. Or, if your students have international penpals, you could perform a reader's theater with them! You can invite classes from another school to be part of the audience as well.

If your classroom uses Zoom or Google Meet, you can send out invites to parents to join the session and watch their children perform the reader's theater "live." As with any videoconference, create a passcode to join the meeting. This will keep your session safe. Make sure that students understand that during the live videoconference, they need to be focused and quiet unless it is their turn to speak. A livestream online will be just like a real-life performance, and students will not have the option to stop or start over. Go over the same expectations and rules of theater with students that you would if they were performing in person.

If a livestream online performance does not work for scheduling purposes, or your students are worried about making mistakes, or even if you just question the reliability of the internet connection, consider prerecording the performance instead. If you record the performance, students may feel more comfortable knowing that they can start over if they make a mistake. (Just remind students that no performance is perfect, and part of theater is just rolling with the mistakes!)

When recording a performance on Zoom (or whichever software you choose), you will typically be given an .MP4 file at the end. This is perfect for uploading to YouTube. You can then provide the link to parents to watch on their own viewing schedule. (Ensure that everything you post online is private and only accessible with the link you provide to students and parents.) You can also choose to drop the .MP4 file into a video-editing program, such as iMovie, and have students assist you with postproduction video editing. Make sure students can access the final-performance video. This will help them with their self-assessment rubrics at the end of each unit.

What Happened to Amelia Earhart?
Lesson Plan

Content Objectives

- Read grade-level text orally with accuracy, appropriate rate, and expression on successive readings.
- Read grade-level text with purpose and understanding.
- Acknowledge differences in the points of view of characters, including by speaking in a different voice for each character when reading dialogue aloud.

Materials

- student copies of *What Happened to Amelia Earhart?* Badge Art (pages 12–13)
- student copies of *What Happened to Amelia Earhart?* Script (pages 14–19)
- student copies of *What Happened to Amelia Earhart?* Activity (page 20)
- student copies of *What Happened to Amelia Earhart?* Journal (page 21)
- highlighters, crayons, markers

Before Reading

1. Begin by assessing students' prior knowledge (if any) of the history of aviation. Ask students if they know who the Wright brothers were. If they don't, tell them that the Wright brothers built the first successful gasoline-powered airplane in 1903. After that, people were excited to learn how to fly. Most pilots in the early 1900s were men. Amelia Earhart was born in 1897. She was fascinated by flight and was determined to set new records. In 1928, she was the first female to cross the Atlantic Ocean by plane. People celebrated her, but she was confused as to why. She merely rode as a passenger on the plane! She wanted to give them something to really celebrate. Four years later, she flew her own plane solo across the Atlantic. This was an accomplishment that she could be proud of.

2. Ask students if anyone has been on an airplane. Allow them to share their experiences. Then, remind students that airplanes in the 1900s were different from how they are today. Big commercial planes that students may have flown on did not exist. Airplanes were much smaller. Many of them had exposed roofs, meaning that pilots had to dress extra warm in order to not freeze at high altitudes. There were no cell phones and no GPS. People had to use paper maps to plan their trips. Vast stretches of the ocean remained uncharted and unknown. Navigators only had radio signals to help them communicate on their trips. Pilots could pick up radio signals broadcasted by ships and fly toward them to set their course of direction.

3. Tell students that they will be performing a reader's theater play about the unsolved mystery of what happened to Amelia Earhart on her last airplane flight. Distribute copies of the script. Assign students their roles based on reading proficiencies. See page 11 for a list of the reading levels for each role in the *What Happened to Amelia Earhart?* script.

What Happened to Amelia Earhart?
Lesson Plan *(cont.)*

Rehearsal

1. Once students have been assigned their parts, tell them to go through the entire script and highlight their parts. Then, give students time to silently read either the entire script or just their highlighted sections. Ask them to use a pencil to underline any words that they do not know or do not know how to pronounce. Go over these words together to ensure understanding.

2. This script has key vocabulary that students may not know. For a fun vocabulary twist, write each of the following words on separate pieces of paper: *aviator, navigator, fuel, radio operators, technology, GPS, route, Morse code.* Hand each student one of the papers. Tell them to fold it into their best paper airplane! Then, have students take turns sailing the vocab-word paper airplane to partners. The partner will unfold it, read the word, and look up the definition. Then, they can read the definition out loud and fly the next vocab-word paper airplane. Repeat until all the words have been defined and understood.

3. Give students time to practice their reader's theater. Remind them to speak with fluency, rate, expression, and tone. They need to play the role of the character using just their voices! Demonstrate reading a few lines in a dull, monotonous tone. Then, read the same lines with expression and ask students to explain the difference. Do the same thing with reading pace (read lines too quickly or too slowly) and then demonstrate a proper pace. Lastly, whisper lines softly. Then, read them again with a proper volume. Ask students if they understand the differences.

Performance

1. There are a variety of ways for your students to perform the *What Happened to Amelia Earhart?* reader's theater. See pages 5–8 for performance ideas.

2. Distribute copies of the badges (pages 12–13). Give students time to decorate their character's badge using crayons or markers.

3. Remind students to speak loudly and clearly and with confidence! Encourage them to show emotion and feeling with their voices. Even the narrators can show emotion by reading their parts with an authoritative and confident tone! If stage fright or public speaking is an issue for some students, remind them to focus on their lines instead of worrying about the audience. And lastly, remind students to take deep breaths, smile, and have fun with this!

Assessment

1. Distribute student copies of the *What Happened to Amelia Earhart?* Activity (page 20). Go over the activity sheet together, and then have students complete it independently.

2. Distribute student copies of the *What Happened to Amelia Earhart?* Journal (page 21). Remind students that the story of Amelia Earhart is still an unsolved mystery. Discuss the possible theories presented in the script, along with any of your own. Then, give students time to journal their theories on what really happened to Amelia and Fred.

What Happened to Amelia Earhart?
Characters

Assigning Characters

The roles in this reader's theater have been leveled to fit the individual needs of your students. When students feel confident in their reading fluency, they will engage with the character and feel comfortable performing in front of others. Remind students that they are performing a play using only their voices. The way they speak each word matters! Demonstrate the difference between monotone reading and reading with fluency and expression so students can understand the expectations.

You might also consider assigning nonspeaking roles to students who are reluctant to read aloud. These students could act as directors or coaches. Remind them that their roles are very important. They will have to know the script extremely well and will be in charge of prompting students when it is their turn to read.

What Happened to Amelia Earhart? has six roles. They are listed here in order of highest reading-level proficiency to lowest.

Grade 3 Reading Levels:

Narrator 1   Played by: _________________________

Narrator 2   Played by: _________________________

Amelia Earhart   Played by: _________________________

Grade 2/High Grade 1 Reading Levels:

News Reporter   Played by: _________________________

Fred Noonan   Played by: _________________________

Radio Operator   Played by: _________________________

What Happened to Amelia Earhart? Badge Art

What Happened to Amelia Earhart? Badge Art (cont.)

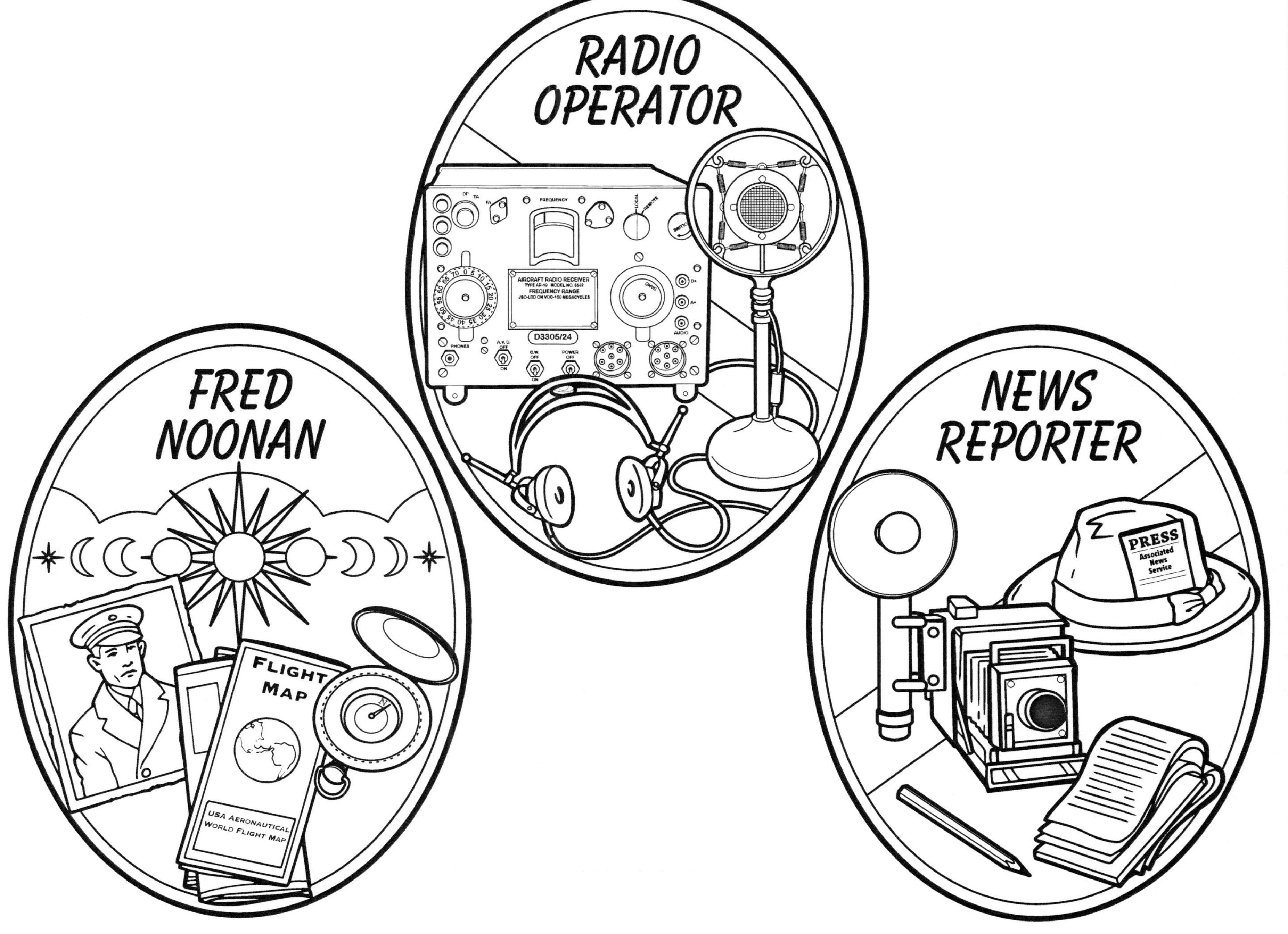

What Happened to Amelia Earhart? Script

Characters
- Narrator 1
- Narrator 2
- Amelia Earhart
- Fred Noonan
- News Reporter
- Radio Operator

Setting

Act 1 takes place at an airport in Miami, Florida. Act 2 takes place inside of Amelia's plane. Her plane is soaring over the Pacific Ocean.

Act 1

Narrator 1: The day is June 1, 1937. Amelia Earhart is talking to a news reporter. They are at the airport.

Narrator 2: Amelia is a famous aviator. That is a person who flies planes. She is ready to take a long trip.

News Reporter: Hello, Amelia! How are you today?

Amelia: I feel great! I am ready to be the first female to fly around the world.

News Reporter: Who is this with you?

Amelia: This is my navigator. He makes sure we don't get lost.

Fred: That is right. I am good at reading maps. My name is Fred.

Amelia: I chose Fred to help me on this journey. I trust his skills! He is experienced at reading maps and has helped me plan our travel path. We have gone over all of the maps to find the best possible route to fly.

Narrator 1: Fred Noonan was also a sailor. He knew how to use the sky to find his way. He used the sun, moon, and stars to guide him.

News Reporter: What is the name of your plane?

What Happened to
Amelia Earhart? Script *(cont.)*

Amelia: My plane is called the Electra. It is a very special plane.

Narrator 2: The Electra was built to fly far. It had extra tanks for fuel. And it had new radios. This helped the pilot talk to the radio operators on the ground.

Fred: This plane will take us around the world!

News Reporter: What if you get lost?

Fred: I always find my way. And we have tools to help us.

News Reporter: Do you get scared?

Amelia: I am never afraid when I am in my plane. I know this trip is dangerous. But I feel confident, and I love to fly! I hope that I can inspire young girls to become pilots. Flying around the globe will be a dream come true for me. I have been waiting my whole life for this moment.

News Reporter: You have already changed the world. Women are learning to fly planes because of you.

Amelia: Thank you! I really hope that girls will see that they can be anything they want to be. The world is changing!

News Reporter: What will this trip be like? Has it been done before?

Fred: We are going to do something new. We are taking the longest route around the world.

Narrator 1: There had been a few flights across the world. But Amelia would be the first female pilot to do this.

Narrator 2: And they were going to fly along the middle of the globe. This would set a new record for distance.

News Reporter: You have many fans. They want to know about your trip. Can you tell us about your journals?

What Happened to
Amelia Earhart? Script *(cont.)*

Amelia: Yes, of course. I keep a journal during my flights and plan to write a book when I return home. I like to write down the things that I see. I also call my husband on the phone at each of our stops. I send him my notes through the mail.

Fred: These notes help people know where we are on the map.

News Reporter: One last question. When did you know you wanted to be a pilot?

Amelia: In 1920, I rode on a plane for the first time. I knew it was what I wanted to do with my life. I signed up for flying lessons as soon as we landed!

News Reporter: Thank you for speaking with us. Good luck! We look forward to your safe return.

Act 2

Fred: The plane is ready to go. We are so close to the end of our trip. Let's take off!

Narrator 1: The trip had been hard. Fred and Amelia made many stops. They also had bad weather along the way.

Narrator 2: And, their plane needed repairs. Amelia also got sick. They had to stay on the ground for five days.

Narrator 1: At last, they were in a city called Lae. They were getting ready for the final part of the trip. It would be the longest. They had to cross the entire Pacific Ocean.

Amelia: Okay, Fred. I am ready too. Did you speak to the radio operators?

Fred: I did. They know our plans. We will land on Howland Island.

What Happened to Amelia Earhart? Script *(cont.)*

Narrator 2: Howland Island was very small. It was hard to see when flying above the ocean. Amelia needed to land there to put more fuel in the plane. The radio operators would help them. They could give directions.

Narrator 1: Things were different back then. Airplanes were new technology. There were no cell phones or GPS. Pilots had to use radio signals to send messages.

Amelia: My plane has enough fuel to fly for 20 hours. It should take us 18 hours to reach Howland Island. We can do this!

Narrator 1: The plane takes off without any problems. Soon they are soaring above the blue ocean waves.

Amelia: Hello, operator? Can you hear us?

Radio Operator: Yes, we can hear you.

Amelia: We are flying slower than we wanted to. But, everything looks good.

Radio Operator: The signal will go out for a bit. We will still be here. Call us soon.

Narrator 2: Radio operators were on a ship at Howland Island. They were waiting to hear from Amelia.

Narrator 1: Seven hours went by. The radio operators were nervous. They could not see Amelia's plane. They had not gotten any calls. But then …

Amelia: Cloudy and overcast!

Radio Operator: Amelia, we can hear you. Loud and clear! Are you okay?

Narrator 2: Amelia sent more radio calls. The operators could hear her. But they soon realized that she could *not* hear them!

What Happened to Amelia Earhart? Script *(cont.)*

Amelia: Hello? Operator? Can you read me? This is Amelia Earhart. Please come in.

Radio Operator: We are trying to help you land. We can't see your plane.

Narrator 1: Amelia kept calling the operators. They responded each time. But she was not getting their messages. The operators tried sending Morse Code. They sent patterns of beeps that stood for letters.

Radio Operator: Beep, beep, beep.

Fred: Listen! I think they are sending us code.

Radio Operator: Beep, beep, beep.

Amelia: I think that is Morse code, but I don't know it. Do you, Fred?

Fred: No, I don't. What are we going to do?

Amelia: We are running low on fuel. Fred, we have to try to land the plane.

Radio Operator: Can you hear us? We are trying to give you directions. We can help you land.

Narrator 2: The radio operators heard the calls. They answered back. But Amelia and Fred could not hear their calls.

Fred: I wonder if they can hear us.

Amelia: I don't know. I am not sure they heard any of our messages. We are going to have to land the plane without their help. I can't see the island. We are going to have to try our best.

Radio Operator: Hello? Hello?

Narrator 1: And then it went silent.

What Happened to Amelia Earhart? Script *(cont.)*

Radio Operator: We tried to find the plane. Our ships were in the water for days. Nothing was found.

News Reporter: Amelia Earhart is missing! Amelia's plane is lost at sea!

Narrator 1: The newspapers wrote about it. The search went on. People listened to the radio. They hoped to hear radio calls from Amelia.

News Reporter: The president is looking for her too!

Narrator 2: President Roosevelt had 1,500 members of the Navy search the Pacific Ocean.

News Reporter: They searched for two weeks. They found nothing. President Roosevelt called off the search.

Narrator 1: So what happened to Amelia Earhart? We may never know. It is still an unsolved mystery.

Narrator 2: There have been lots of theories. Some people think she landed the plane on the wrong island. Others think the plane crashed into the ocean.

Narrator 1: Some people think Amelia was a spy! They think she may have been taken prisoner. Others think she landed safely and changed her name. They claim she wanted to disappear.

Narrator 2: We only know that Amelia, Fred, and the plane disappeared that day. And they have never been found.

News Reporter: What do *you* think happened?

What Happened to Amelia Earhart? Activity

1. Think about what you learned about Amelia Earhart. List three words you would use to describe her.

____

2. What is an *aviator*?

____

3. How has technology changed since Amelia's flight?

____

____

4. Amelia loved adventure. What is an adventure you would like to take one day?

____

____

____

Reader's Theater Reflections

Think about your performance. Color in the number of stars to show how well you did in each area.

Accuracy: I read my part correctly.	☆ ☆ ☆
Rate: I read at a pace that was not too fast or too slow.	☆ ☆ ☆
Expression: I read my character's part with feeling and emotion.	☆ ☆ ☆

List one way that you can improve your reader's theater performance.

____

____

What Happened to Amelia Earhart? Journal

Amelia, Fred, and the plane disappeared on July 2, 1937. They were never found. The mystery remains unsolved. What do you think happened?

The Hidden Mine Lesson Plan

Content Objectives

- Read grade-level text orally with accuracy, appropriate rate, and expression on successive readings.
- Read grade-level text with purpose and understanding.
- Acknowledge differences in the points of view of characters, including by speaking in a different voice for each character when reading dialogue aloud.

Materials

- student copies of *The Hidden Mine* Badge Art (pages 25–26)
- student copies of *The Hidden Mine* Script (pages 27–32)
- student copies of *The Hidden Mine* Activity (page 33)
- student copies of *The Hidden Mine* Journal (page 34)
- highlighters, crayons, markers
- notecards and dice for vocabulary game

Before Reading

1. Begin by assessing students' prior knowledge (if any) of the history of the gold rush in America. In the mid 1800s, Americans traveled farther west in search of gold, silver, and gems. Mine towns were set up quickly so people could trade and interact with one another. There is a legend in Arizona about a prospector named Jacob Waltz. He was born in Germany but came to America to make a fortune. There are stories of him traveling into the Superstition Mountains and returning with gold. He never told anyone where the gold came from until his final days. And even then, he only gave his friend Julia a riddle and clues but no real map. A hundred years later, a set of carved stones called the Peralta Stones were found in Arizona. The carvings show symbols including a heart, a horse, and a priest. People believe these are a map to Jacob's hidden mine. The stones are on display at the Arizona Museum of Natural History. There is still debate over their authenticity and whether or not they have anything to do with the hidden mine.

2. Tell students that they will be performing a reader's theater play about the unsolved mystery of Jacob Waltz's hidden mine. Distribute copies of the script. Assign students their roles based on reading proficiencies. See page 24 for a list of the reading levels for each role in *The Hidden Mine* script.

The Hidden Mine **Lesson Plan** *(cont.)*

Rehearsal

1. Once students have been assigned their parts, tell them to go through the entire script and highlight their parts. Then, give students time to silently read either the entire script or just their highlighted sections. Ask them to use a pencil and underline any words that they do not know or do not know how to pronounce. Go over these words together to ensure understanding.

2. This script has key vocabulary that students may not know. Consider playing a vocabulary game. Have students sit with partners. Write the following words from the play on notecards: *prosperous, prospector, museum, archeologist, geologist, compass, fortune, quartz, legend, generous.* Each student will take turns reading a word on a notecard. Then, they will give the definition. If they do not know, they can look it up. Then, they will roll the dice and write down the number they scored. Partners go back and forth until all words have been defined. Then, they total their scores to see who wins!

3. Give students time to practice their reader's theater. Remind them to speak with fluency, rate, expression, and tone. They need to play the role of the character using just their voices! Demonstrate reading a few lines in a dull, monotonous tone. Then, read the same lines with expression and ask students to explain the difference. Do the same thing with reading pace (read lines too quickly or too slowly) and then demonstrate a proper pace. Lastly, whisper lines softly. Then, read them again with a proper volume. Ask students if they understand the differences.

Performance

1. There are a variety of ways for your students to perform *The Hidden Mine* reader's theater. See pages 5–8 for performance ideas.

2. Distribute copies of the badges (pages 25–26). Give students time to decorate their character's badge using crayons or markers.

3. Remind students to speak loudly and clearly and with confidence! Encourage them to show emotion and feeling with their voices. Even the narrators can show emotion by reading their parts with an authoritative and confident tone! If stage fright or public speaking is an issue for some students, remind them to focus on their lines instead of worrying about the audience. And lastly, remind students to take a deep breath, smile, and have fun with this!

Assessment

1. Distribute student copies of *The Hidden Mine* Activity (page 33). Go over the activity sheet together and then have students complete it independently.

2. Distribute student copies of *The Hidden Mine* Journal (page 34). Remind students that the location of Jacob's mine is still an unsolved mystery. Discuss the possible theories presented in the script, along with any of your own. Then, give students time to journal their theories.

The Hidden Mine Characters

Assigning Characters

The roles in this reader's theater have been leveled to fit the individual needs of your students. When students feel confident in their reading fluency, they will engage with the character and feel comfortable performing in front of others. Remind students that they are performing a play using only their voices. The way they speak each word matters! Demonstrate the difference between monotone reading and reading with fluency and expression so students can understand the expectations.

You might also consider assigning nonspeaking roles to students who are reluctant to read aloud. These students could act as directors or coaches. Remind them that their roles are very important. They will have to know the script extremely well and will be in charge of prompting students when it is their turn to read.

The Hidden Mine has six roles. They are listed here in order of highest reading-level proficiency to lowest.

Grade 3 Reading Levels:

Narrator 1   Played by: _______________________________________

Narrator 2   Played by: _______________________________________

Joe   Played by: _______________________________________

Grade 2/High Grade 1 Reading Levels:

Maria   Played by: _______________________________________

Jacob Waltz   Played by: _______________________________________

Julia Thomas   Played by: _______________________________________

The Hidden Mine Badge Art

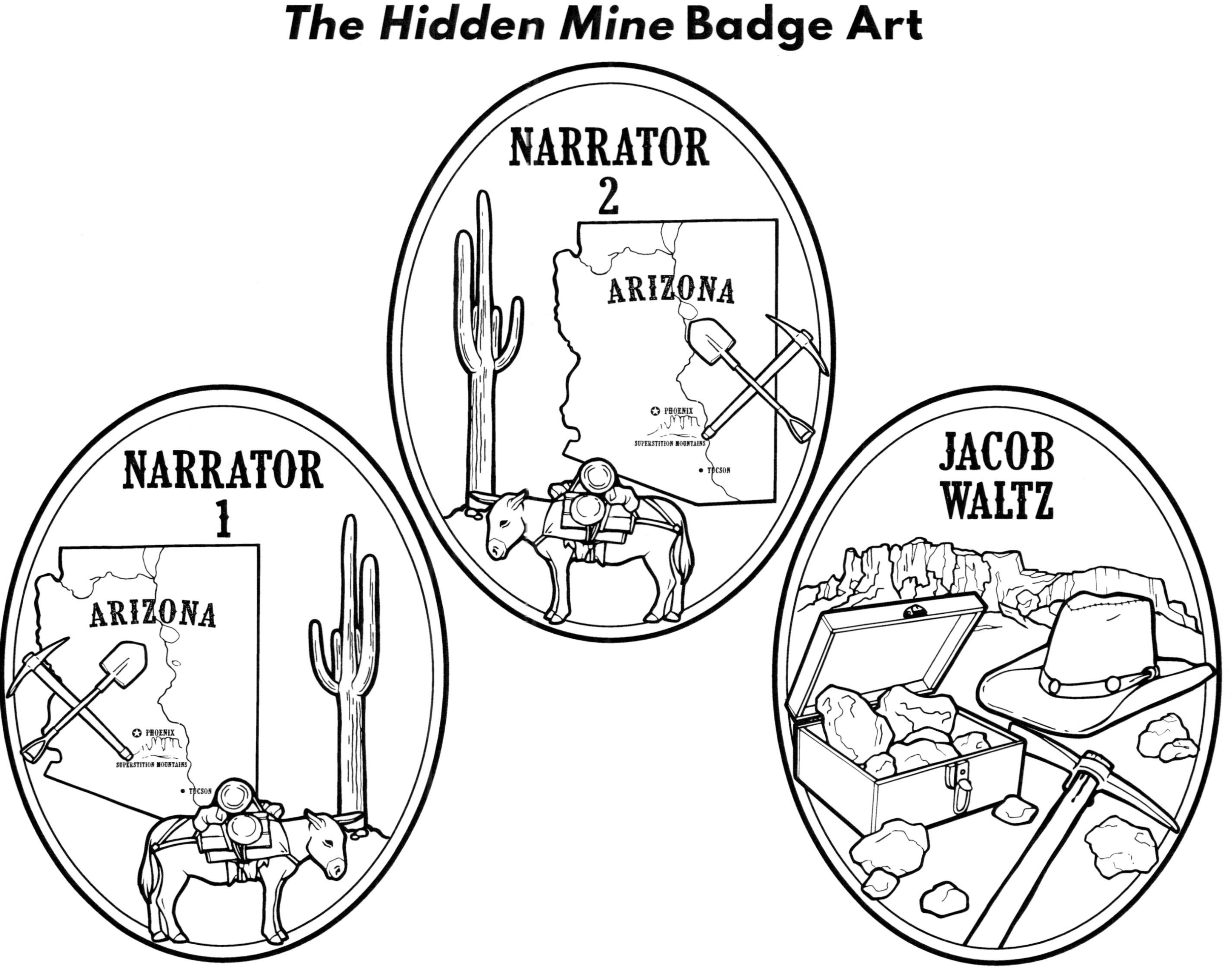

The Hidden Mine Badge Art *(cont.)*

The Hidden Mine Script

Characters

- Jacob Waltz
- Julia Thomas
- Joe
- Maria
- Narrator 1
- Narrator 2

Setting

Act 1 takes place in Julia Thomas's house in 1891. Act 2 takes place along a dirt trail in Arizona.

Act 1

Jacob: [*yawns loudly*]

Julia: How are you feeling, Jacob? You look tired.

Jacob: I must admit, I have been better. I am an old man, Julia.

Julia: You have lived a prosperous life, Jacob. Full of luck and fortune.

Narrator 1: The year is 1891. Jacob Waltz is on his deathbed. His friend Julia is taking care of him at her house. Julia owns a bakery in town. She was worried about Jacob. He did not have any friends or family to take care of him.

Narrator 2: Jacob lived a long and mysterious life. He was born in Germany but came to America in search of wealth. He wanted to strike it rich!

Narrator 1: This time in history was called the gold rush. People kept moving west across America. They were looking for gold, silver, and quartz.

Narrator 2: Jacob moved to Arizona and spent many years as a prospector. This is a person who mines for gold and gems.

Narrator 1: Legend says that Jacob paid for everything with pure pieces of gold. But nobody knew where he found the gold. He kept it a secret.

Narrator 2: A secret until his last day.

Jacob: [*coughs*]

The Hidden Mine Script *(cont.)*

Julia: Jacob, you don't look so well.

Jacob: I think my luck has finally run out. But I have something I want to tell you. We have been friends for a long time. Have you ever wondered where I get my gold?

Julia: Well, yes. Everybody wonders how you became rich. But you have never told anyone your secrets.

Jacob: Years ago, I found a mine. It is in the Superstition Mountains. It is full of gold.

Julia: But where? That mountain range is huge!

Narrator 1: Jacob's hidden mine could be anywhere. The Superstition Mountain range spans across 242 square miles.

Jacob: Look under the bed. Do you see that box? Open it.

Narrator 2: Julia looked under the bed and found a small box. She opened it and gasped.

Julia: [*gasping*] Jacob Waltz! Is this real gold?

Narrator 1: Julia was staring at a large gold nugget. It was solid and heavy.

Julia: Is this all that is left from your hidden mine?

Jacob: Not even close! That is just what is left from my last trip. There is plenty more where that came from. But it is quite a journey. I am too old to return to the mine.

Julia: Jacob, what are you going to do with all of your gold?

Jacob: I would like to give this gold nugget to you. And I want to tell you how to find the mine. I do not need to keep it a secret any longer.

Julia: That is very generous of you. I appreciate it.

The Hidden Mine Script *(cont.)*

Jacob: I don't have any family. I want to thank you for taking care of me in my old age. You can keep all of the gold you find in the mine. But you have to find it first. The mine is not easy to locate.

Julia: Give me one minute. I would like to write everything down. Maybe I can try to draw a map.

Narrator 1: Julia grabbed an ink pen and a piece of paper.

Narrator 2: But Jacob did not give her directions. He did not show her how to draw a map. Instead, he gave her a riddle.

Jacob: [*reading slowly*]
No miner will find my mine. To find my mine, you must pass a cow barn. From my mine, you can see the military trail. But from the military trail, you cannot see my mine. The rays of the setting sun shine into the entrance of my mine. There is a trick in the trail to my mine. My mine is located in a north-trending canyon. There is a rock face on the trail to my mine.

Julia: Jacob, is this a joke? How will that help me find the mine?

Narrator 1: But Jacob was already fast asleep.

Narrator 2: Julia wrote down every word. She tried to draw a map using the riddle. After Jacob passed away, Julia decided to sell her bakery. She spent years seeking the hidden mine. She never found it.

Narrator 1: Julia told her story to people. She even sold copies of the maps she drew. She hoped that someone would one day find Jacob's hidden mine. Julia's stories started a legend that remains today.

Act 2

Maria: Boy, it sure is hot today!

Joe: Welcome to the Superstition Mountains. It's always too hot or too cold!

The Hidden Mine Script *(cont.)*

Narrator 1: Maria works at a museum in the city. She is an archeologist. Her museum has a set of stones called the Peralta Stones. They are stones engraved with symbols and letters. Some people think they are a map to Jacob Waltz's hidden mine. Maria wants to learn more about them.

Narrator 2: So Maria asked Joe if he would take her on a tour of the Superstition Mountains.

Maria: So, Geologist Joe, tell me all you know about the Peralta Stones. Are they really a treasure map?

Joe: [*laughs*] Well, Maria, I am not sure I believe they are much of anything. I had a chance to look at the stones up close. They used to be in a local museum here. Some people think the stones are a map to Jacob's gold mine. But I think they are fake.

Maria: Why do you think that?

Joe: The stones are just carved pieces of sandstone. But it looks like they were carved with modern tools. I don't think they are as old as some people think. The images are things like a horse, a priest, and a heart. It says if you find the heart, you will find the gold. But to this day, no one has ever found the gold.

Maria: Hmmmm. What about the riddle left behind by Mr. Waltz?

Joe: Aha! Is that why you asked if I would take you on a tour of this mountain range? Are you in search of the hidden mine?

Maria: Not exactly. I am fascinated by old things. I also want to learn as much as I can about the stones. People like to ask a lot of questions about them at the museum.

The Hidden Mine Script *(cont.)*

Narrator 2: Joe and Maria are hiking along a trail. Joe is a geologist. He studies rocks. He lives in Arizona. He has been studying different minerals and rocks along the Superstition Mountains for years.

Joe: Well, I don't know what else I can tell you about the stones. Many locals believe they were carved by a member of the Peralta family. And some legends say that Jacob's hidden mine was once owned by the Peralta family.

Maria: Oh, so that's the connection. I grew up hearing stories about the hidden mine. I even memorized Jacob's riddle. "No miner will find my mine. To find my mine, you must pass a cow barn. From my mine, you can see the military trail. But from the military trail, you cannot see my mine. The rays of the setting sun shine into the entrance of my mine. There is a trick in the trail to my mine. My mine is located in a north-trending canyon. There is a rock face on the trail to my mine."

Joe: I haven't heard that riddle in a long time! There is a large rock off one of the trails. It looks like it has a face. That could be what Jacob meant.

Maria: How exciting! Maybe it really does exist.

Joe: My opinion is that the mine really does exist. I had a chance to see the famous gold nugget. You know, the one Jacob gave to Julia over a hundred years ago! It seems very likely that it did come from somewhere out here.

Maria: But why has it been so hard to find the hidden mine? It is such a popular legend.

Joe: These mountains are a mysterious place, Maria. To start, most people treasure-hunt with a compass. But that doesn't work out here. There are too many magnetic rocks. They mess with the compasses.

Maria: Oh wow. What about cell phones?

Joe: There is no cell phone service out here in the desert. If you get lost or hurt, nobody can find you. That makes it a dangerous journey.

The Hidden Mine Script *(cont.)*

Maria: And I imagine it can get very hot out here.

Joe: That's the problem with the desert. It is very hot during the day. People hike in short sleeves. But the temperature drops as soon as the sun sets. It can get very cold at night! Sometimes there are storms even in the summer.

Maria: I see. This mysterious legend is making more sense to me now. Thank you, Joe. I am so glad I had a chance to see this area for myself. I have a feeling Jacob's mine may remain hidden forever!

Joe: People love a good treasure hunt! I am positive that there is gold left to find in these mountains.

Maria: Well, you are an expert in rocks. I think you're right! Do you mind if I take a photograph to display in my museum?

Joe: Go right ahead. It sure is beautiful out here, isn't it?

Maria: Beautiful and mysterious!

Narrator 1: Jacob Waltz's mine is still considered an unsolved mystery. There have been many treasure hunters over the years. Some people claim they have found it! But all the claims point to different spots in the mountain range. And so far, no one has had real proof of their findings.

Jacob: Ha, ha! The world may never know my secret!

Narrator 2: Maybe one day there will be proof! All it takes is for a treasure hunter to find gold that matches the pieces left by Jacob.

Narrator 1: Or, maybe the mine doesn't exist at all. Maybe Jacob wanted to tell a tale so that his legend would live on forever.

Narrator 2: What do *you* think?

The Hidden Mine Activity

1. Why did many people move west during the gold rush?

____

____

2. What is a *prospector*?

____

____

3. Why does Joe think the Peralta Stones are fake?

____

____

4. Would you ever want to search for the hidden mine? Why or why not?

____

____

____

Reader's Theater Reflections

Think about your performance. Color in the number of stars to show how well you did in each area.

Accuracy: I read my part correctly.	☆ ☆ ☆
Rate: I read at a pace that was not too fast or too slow.	☆ ☆ ☆
Expression: I read my character's part with feeling and emotion.	☆ ☆ ☆

List one way that you can improve your reader's theater performance.

____

____

The Hidden Mine Journal

Jacob Waltz lived over a hundred years ago. Many people claim to have found his hidden mine. But no one has real proof. It remains an unsolved mystery. Do you think the mine is still hidden? Or was it all just a made-up story? Explain.

The Hidden Mine

The Escape Lesson Plan

Content Objectives

- Read grade-level text orally with accuracy, appropriate rate, and expression on successive readings.
- Read grade-level text with purpose and understanding.
- Acknowledge differences in the points of view of characters, including by speaking in a different voice for each character when reading dialogue aloud.

Materials

- student copies of *The Escape* Badge Art (pages 38–39)
- student copies of *The Escape* Script (pages 40–45)
- student copies of *The Escape* Activity (page 46)
- student copies of *The Escape* Journal (page 47)
- highlighters, crayons, markers

Before Reading

1. Begin by assessing students' prior knowledge (if any) of Alcatraz Island. It is a popular tourist destination in San Francisco, California. It is located 1.25 miles from San Francisco in San Francisco Bay and is only a little over 20 acres in size. Alcatraz is known for its prison, which was open from 1934 to 1963. It was thought to be an inescapable fortress, mostly because the water was freezing and the currents were very strong. There were 36 prisoners over time who tried to escape and none were successful. That is, until three prisoners attempted an escape in 1962. Frank Morris and brothers John and Clarence Anglin successfully got off the island. But there is little proof that they survived the water and made it safely to shore. The case remains an unsolved mystery.

2. Give students some more fun facts to get them thinking about life on Alcatraz Island. It wasn't just home to a prison. The workers, guards, and their families could also live on the island. They had a bowling alley, an ice-cream shop, and a market. But there were also daily boat rides to the city throughout the day. Today, there is a swim competition called the Alcatraz Triathlon. While it is difficult, it does prove that it is possible to swim to shore from the island.

3. Tell students that they will be performing a reader's theater play about the unsolved mystery of three prisoners who escaped from Alcatraz. Distribute copies of the script. Assign students their roles based on reading proficiencies. See page 37 for a list of the reading levels for each role in *The Escape* script.

The Escape Lesson Plan *(cont.)*

Rehearsal

1. Once students have been assigned their parts, tell them to go through the entire script and highlight their parts. Then, give students time to silently read either the entire script or just their highlighted sections. Ask them to use a pencil and underline any words that they do not know or do not know how to pronounce. Go over these words together to ensure understanding.

2. This script has key vocabulary that students may not know. Consider playing a vocabulary game or creating a word wall. Write the following words from the play on the board or a piece of chart paper: *genius, vents, accordion, dummy, promising, tides, current, investigate, analysis, evidence, mysterious, inconclusive.* Ask students to help you define each one. Write the definitions next to the words. If students are unsure of the definitions, have them read the dictionary definition to you.

3. Give students time to practice their reader's theater. Remind them to speak with fluency, rate, expression, and tone. They need to play the role of the character using just their voices! Demonstrate reading a few lines in a dull, monotonous tone. Then, read the same lines with expression and ask students to explain the difference. Do the same thing with reading pace (read lines too quickly or too slowly) and then demonstrate a proper pace. Lastly, whisper lines softly. Then, read them again with a proper volume. Ask students if they understand the differences.

Performance

1. There are a variety of ways for your students to perform *The Escape* reader's theater. See pages 5–8 for performance ideas.

2. Distribute copies of the badges (pages 38–39). Give students time to decorate their character's badge using crayons or markers.

3. Remind students to speak loudly and clearly and with confidence! Encourage them to show emotion and feeling with their voices. Even the narrators can show emotion by reading their parts with an authoritative and confident tone! If stage fright or public speaking is an issue for some students, remind them to focus on their lines instead of worrying about the audience. And lastly, remind students to take a deep breath, smile, and have fun with this!

Assessment

1. Distribute student copies of *The Escape* Activity (page 46). Go over the activity sheet together and then have students complete it independently.

2. Distribute student copies of *The Escape* Journal (page 47). Remind students that the location of the three prisoners is still an unsolved mystery. Discuss the possible theories presented in the script, along with any of your own. Then, give students time to journal their theories.

The Escape Characters

Assigning Characters

The roles in this reader's theater have been leveled to fit the individual needs of your students. When students feel confident in their reading fluency, they will engage with the character and feel comfortable performing in front of others. Remind students that they are performing a play using only their voices. The way they speak each word matters! Demonstrate the difference between monotone reading and reading with fluency and expression so students can understand the expectations.

You might also consider assigning nonspeaking roles to students who are reluctant to read aloud. These students could act as directors or coaches. Remind them that their role is very important. They will have to know the script extremely well and will be in charge of prompting students when it is their turn to read.

The Escape has six roles. They are listed here in order of highest reading-level proficiency to lowest.

Grade 3 Reading Levels:

Narrator   Played by: _______________________________

FBI Agent Morris   Played by: _______________________________

FBI Agent Smith   Played by: _______________________________

Grade 2/High Grade 1 Reading Levels:

Frank Morris   Played by: _______________________________

John Anglin   Played by: _______________________________

Clarence Anglin   Played by: _______________________________

The Escape Badge Art

The Escape Badge Art (cont.)

The Escape

The Escape Script

Characters
- Frank Morris
- John Anglin
- Clarence Anglin
- Agent Smith
- Agent Morris
- Narrator

Setting

Act 1 takes place at Alcatraz prison in 1962. Act 2 takes place in a San Francisco police department.

Act 1

Frank: Pssst! Hey, John! Are you awake?

John: Barely. It's late, Frank. What do you want?

Frank: I have an idea. It's a good one. I'm going to break out of this place.

John: That is impossible and you know it. We are on Alcatraz Island. No one has ever escaped. We are surrounded by water.

Frank: Yeah, well, like I said earlier. I have a plan. And it's a good one. I know it will work. Are you with me?

John: Let's talk about it in the morning. We can talk to my brother about it too. Get some sleep.

Narrator: Frank Morris and brothers John and Clarence Anglin were in prison. The prison was called Alcatraz. It was on an island in the middle of the San Francisco Bay. Alcatraz was thought to be the one prison that was *impossible* to escape from.

Clarence: [*yawning*] Good morning, brother. How did you sleep?

John: Terrible. Frank kept talking all night in the prison cell next to me. He was going on and on about a plan.

Clarence: A plan? Like an escape plan?

John: Yes. But I told him it's impossible.

The Escape Script *(cont.)*

Clarence: Nothing is impossible, John. I want to hear more about it.

Narrator: Frank was in prison for bank robbery. He was known for being a genius. If anyone could come up with an escape plan, it was Frank. Later that day, Frank told the Anglin brothers about his plan for escape.

Frank: I have studied every part of this prison. We will only have one chance at getting out. In order for it to work, we need every detail to be perfect. This is going to take a lot of work. But I can't do it alone. Are you with me?

Clarence: We've got nothing to lose, John. Let's see if we can break out of the unbreakable prison.

John: Let's get to work. What do we need to do first?

Frank: Okay, this is the plan. I have been working on making a drill. I took apart a vacuum cleaner when I was on cleaning duty. The motor will power my drill. If we drill a hole in our cell wall, we can escape through the vents. The vents will take us to the roof. Then, we slide down to the ground.

John: Whoa, wait a minute. How are we going to drill without them hearing it?

Frank: Well, I play my accordion every night. We will just time it right. You drill while I play. That solves that problem.

Clarence: We can't swim to shore. The water is freezing, and it is too far. We don't have a raft.

Frank: Leave that up to me. I can build a raft out of raincoats. And, I can inflate the raft using my accordion! I think we should head toward Angel Island. That is only two miles from here. We should be able to find new clothes there.

John: Frank, you are a genius!

The Escape Script *(cont.)*

Clarence: But what about when they make the rounds at night to check our cells? If we're gone, they will look for us right away. We won't have enough time to make it all the way out.

Frank: We build dummies! I can create fake heads using toilet paper and soap and water. I'll collect hair off the floor in the barbershop to glue on top. I'll even paint them to look just like us!

John: This plan does sound promising.

Frank: Guys, I have thought about everything. Trust me. It's going to work. But only if we follow the plan exactly. I have been studying the tides in the bay. There is a strong current. Our best chance is to get into the water between 11 p.m. and midnight.

Narrator: Frank's plan was set into motion. Each night, John drilled a hole in the wall while Frank played his accordion. The guards never heard a sound. The men planned their escape for June 11, 1962.

Frank: Tonight is the night. Are you guys ready for this? I made us life vests just in case my raft fails. But I think everything is going to work out.

Clarence: My dummy head is ready. It really does look real! I even stuffed my bed with extra clothes to look like my body.

John: My dummy is ready too. What happens once we get through the vents and meet on the roof?

Frank: I have our raft waiting for us by the shore. We will need to climb down from the roof. We also have to climb over a fence. But freedom awaits!

Clarence: So we wait until the lights are out. The last bed check is at 9 p.m. And then Frank will whisper when it's time.

John: We need to move quickly. I am nervous about the guards seeing us.

The Escape Script *(cont.)*

Frank: I have timed everything out. Don't worry. But remember the most important part. Once we get off this island, life will be different. They will look for us. You need to stay invisible.

Clarence: We can stick together.

John: It will be a second chance to start over.

Narrator: That night, the three men disappeared without a trace! The guards did not suspect anything. The men were not seen during the escape. Early in the morning, the guards realized the men were gone. They sent out a search team. The raft later washed ashore. No bodies were ever found. The FBI investigated. They looked through the water. They believed that the men drowned in the water. That seemed to be the end of the case. But then, something interesting happened.

Act 2

Agent Smith: So what do you think about this letter? It's probably fake, right?

Agent Morris: All I know is that the San Francisco Police Department called us. They want our help with the investigation. I thought the Alcatraz case was closed. I guess they kept it open.

Agent Smith: It's been so long, though! Those three prisoners broke out 50 years ago. Even if they are alive, they would be old men.

Agent Morris: Plus, you would think that someone would have spotted them. Or maybe they would have visited their families.

Agent Smith: Well, maybe they left the country. It seems like the only way they could get away with it.

Agent Morris: I think that's possible. But, the police always said they were probably swept out to the Pacific Ocean. I am not sure they even made it to land. But no one really knows anything for sure.

The Escape Script *(cont.)*

Narrator: Agent Smith and Agent Morris work for the FBI. This is a department in the government. They investigate important cases. A mysterious letter showed up at the police department. The police called the FBI to check it out.

Agent Smith: I remember reading about the Alcatraz escape when I was a kid. I bet they really did escape.

Agent Morris: My dad grew up here in San Francisco. He said there were stories about the Anglin brothers. And Frank Morris was a legend. He was believed to have an IQ of 133! That is very smart. My dad believes that they made it out of the bay alive.

Agent Smith: Does he think they swam? Or paddled on a raft?

Agent Morris: He has a different theory. He thinks that Frank timed it just right. There was a boat that took workers from Alcatraz across the bay. He thinks they got on a raft and held onto a rope. The rope was attached to this boat. They just had to hold on as the boat pulled them to shore.

Agent Smith: Wow! I never heard that before. It seems believable. Plus, they never found them in the water.

Agent Morris: Anything is possible. Let's take a look at the new evidence.

Narrator: The agents arrive at the San Francisco Police Department. They receive some new evidence. It seems to prove that the three men really did escape Alcatraz.

Agent Smith: So here's the letter. Let me read it out loud: "My name is John Anglin. I escaped from Alcatraz in June 1962 with my brother Clarence and Frank Morris. I'm 83 years old and in bad shape. I have cancer. Yes, we all made it that night, but barely."

Agent Morris: Why would he send that letter to the police department?

Agent Smith: The letter goes on. John asks for the police to announce it on TV. He promises to go to jail for one year if they will give him medicine.

The Escape Script *(cont.)*

Agent Morris: That sounds like a joke. Why would we announce that on TV?

Agent Smith: I have no idea. It does sound strange.

Narrator: The letter was sent to be analyzed. They looked at the handwriting. They compared it to the handwriting samples from John before he went to Alcatraz. The results were inconclusive. This means that they weren't sure if the handwriting really was from John.

Agent Morris: There is something else too. The Anglin family says that John and Clarence did escape and moved to Brazil. They claim they don't have contact with them. But there are a few things that make them think they are still alive.

Narrator: A photograph of John and Clarence turned up as a new piece of evidence. Relatives say it is a real photo of the brothers. Computer analysis studied the faces in the photo. Then it compared the faces to older photos of the brothers. It seems likely that they are the same. But it's not completely certain. The men in the photo are wearing sunglasses. This blocks part of their faces. So there is no way to prove that it *really* is them.

Agent Smith: Let's look at the photograph. It was submitted as evidence. What do you think?

Agent Morris: Gosh, it's hard to say. I think there is a good chance they did make it out of the bay. But their story is so famous. This letter and photo could be fake. It could just be people trying to keep the legend alive.

Agent Smith: You're right. I still think we should keep the case open. We need a little more time. Maybe we can speak to the Anglin family.

Narrator: There are many theories about the escape from Alcatraz. But even today, nothing is certain. What really happened to Frank, John, and Clarence? It remains an unsolved mystery. What do *you* think happened?

The Escape Activity

1. Why did people think it was impossible to escape from Alcatraz?

2. Why was timing so important in the prison escape?

3. What new evidence did the FBI agents study?

4. Do you think the FBI will ever close the case? Why or why not?

Reader's Theater Reflections

Think about your performance. Color in the number of stars to show how well you did in each area.

Accuracy: I read my part correctly.	☆ ☆ ☆
Rate: I read at a pace that was not too fast or too slow.	☆ ☆ ☆
Expression: I read my character's part with feeling and emotion.	☆ ☆ ☆

List one way that you can improve your reader's theater performance.

The Escape Journal

The escape from Alcatraz took place 50 years ago. No one knows what happened after the three men got on the raft. It remains an unsolved mystery. What do you think happened?

The Ghost Ship Lesson Plan

Content Objectives

- Read grade-level text orally with accuracy, appropriate rate, and expression on successive readings.
- Read grade-level text with purpose and understanding.
- Acknowledge differences in the points of view of characters, including by speaking in a different voice for each character when reading dialogue aloud.

Materials

- student copies of *The Ghost Ship* Badge Art (pages 51–52)
- student copies of *The Ghost Ship* Script (pages 53–58)
- student copies of *The Ghost Ship* Activity (page 59)
- student copies of *The Ghost Ship* Journal (page 60)
- highlighters, crayons, markers
- notecards for vocabulary game

Before Reading

1. Begin by assessing students' prior knowledge (if any) of the mystery of the *Mary Celeste*. Tell students that in 1872, a ship called the *Dei Gratia* was sailing through the Atlantic Ocean, 1,000 miles west of Portugal. The crew of sailors was led by Captain David Morehouse and First Mate Oliver Deveau. They were surprised to see an abandoned ship sailing along the ocean. When they got close enough to the ship, Captain David recognized that it was his friend's ship, the *Mary Celeste*. They anchored close to it, and Oliver boarded the ship with a few crew members. He stumbled upon an unsolved mystery! The *Mary Celeste* had a crew of ten people that included the captain's wife and young daughter. But the crew had vanished. All of their things were left behind. The ship still had supplies, food, and clothing. The bottom cabins of the ship were flooded with less than four feet of water, but this wasn't enough to sink the ship. They found a pump that had been taken apart. This might be a clue that the pumps on the ship were not working correctly. The lifeboat was gone. There was no sign of any disaster, and everything on the ship was neat and in order. No captain would abandon a seaworthy ship. What happened remains a mystery!

2. Tell students that they will be performing a reader's theater play about the unsolved mystery of the ghost ship *Mary Celeste*. Distribute copies of the script. Assign students their roles based on reading proficiencies. See page 50 for a list of the reading levels for each role in *The Ghost Ship* script.

The Ghost Ship Lesson Plan *(cont.)*

Rehearsal

1. Once students have been assigned their parts, tell them to go through the entire script and highlight their parts. Then, give students time to silently read either the entire script or just their highlighted sections. Ask them to use a pencil and underline any words that they do not know or do not know how to pronounce. Go over these words together to ensure understanding.

2. This script has key vocabulary that students may not know. Consider playing a vocabulary memory game. Write the following words from the play on separate notecards: *navigation, spyglass, cursed, abandoned, mutiny, investigate, vanished, lifeboat, galley, logbook, rigging, documentaries, salvage reward, oceanographer.* Then, write the definition of each word on separate notecards. Place all the cards facedown. Have students take turns flipping two cards over. If they match a word with the definition, they get to keep the cards. Play until all of the cards have been matched.

3. Give students time to practice their reader's theater. Remind them to speak with fluency, rate, expression, and tone. They need to play the role of the character using just their voices! Demonstrate reading a few lines in a dull, monotonous tone. Then, read the same lines with expression and ask students to explain the difference. Do the same thing with reading pace (read lines too quickly or too slowly) and then demonstrate a proper pace. Lastly, whisper lines softly. Then, read them again with a proper volume. Ask students if they understand the differences.

Performance

1. There are a variety of ways for your students to perform *The Ghost Ship* reader's theater. See pages 5–8 for performance ideas.

2. Distribute copies of the badges (pages 51–52). Give students time to decorate their character's badge using crayons or markers.

3. Remind students to speak loudly and clearly and with confidence! Encourage them to show emotion and feeling with their voices. Even the narrators can show emotion by reading their parts with an authoritative and confident tone! If stage fright or public speaking is an issue for some students, remind them to focus on their lines instead of worrying about the audience. And lastly, remind students to take a deep breath, smile, and have fun with this!

Assessment

1. Distribute student copies of *The Ghost Ship* Activity (page 59). Go over the activity sheet together and then have students complete it independently.

2. Distribute student copies of *The Ghost Ship* Journal (page 60). Remind students that the missing crew on the *Mary Celeste* is still an unsolved mystery. Discuss the possible theories presented in the script, along with any of your own. Then, give students time to journal their theories.

The Ghost Ship Characters

Assigning Characters

The roles in this reader's theater have been leveled to fit the individual needs of your students. When students feel confident in their reading fluency, they will engage with the character and feel comfortable performing in front of others. Remind students that they are performing a play using only their voices. The way they speak each word matters! Demonstrate the difference between monotone reading and reading with fluency and expression so students can understand the expectations.

You might also consider assigning nonspeaking roles to students who are reluctant to read aloud. These students could act as directors or coaches. Remind them that their role is very important. They will have to know the script extremely well and will be in charge of prompting students when it is their turn to read.

The Ghost Ship has six roles. They are listed here in order of highest reading-level proficiency to lowest.

Grade 3 Reading Levels:

Narrator 2   Played by: _______________________________

Anne MacGregor   Played by: _______________________________

Phil Richardson   Played by: _______________________________

Grade 2/High Grade 1 Reading Levels:

Narrator 1   Played by: _______________________________

Captain David Morehouse Played by: _______________________________

Oliver Deveau   Played by: _______________________________

The Ghost Ship Badge Art

The Ghost Ship Badge Art (cont.)

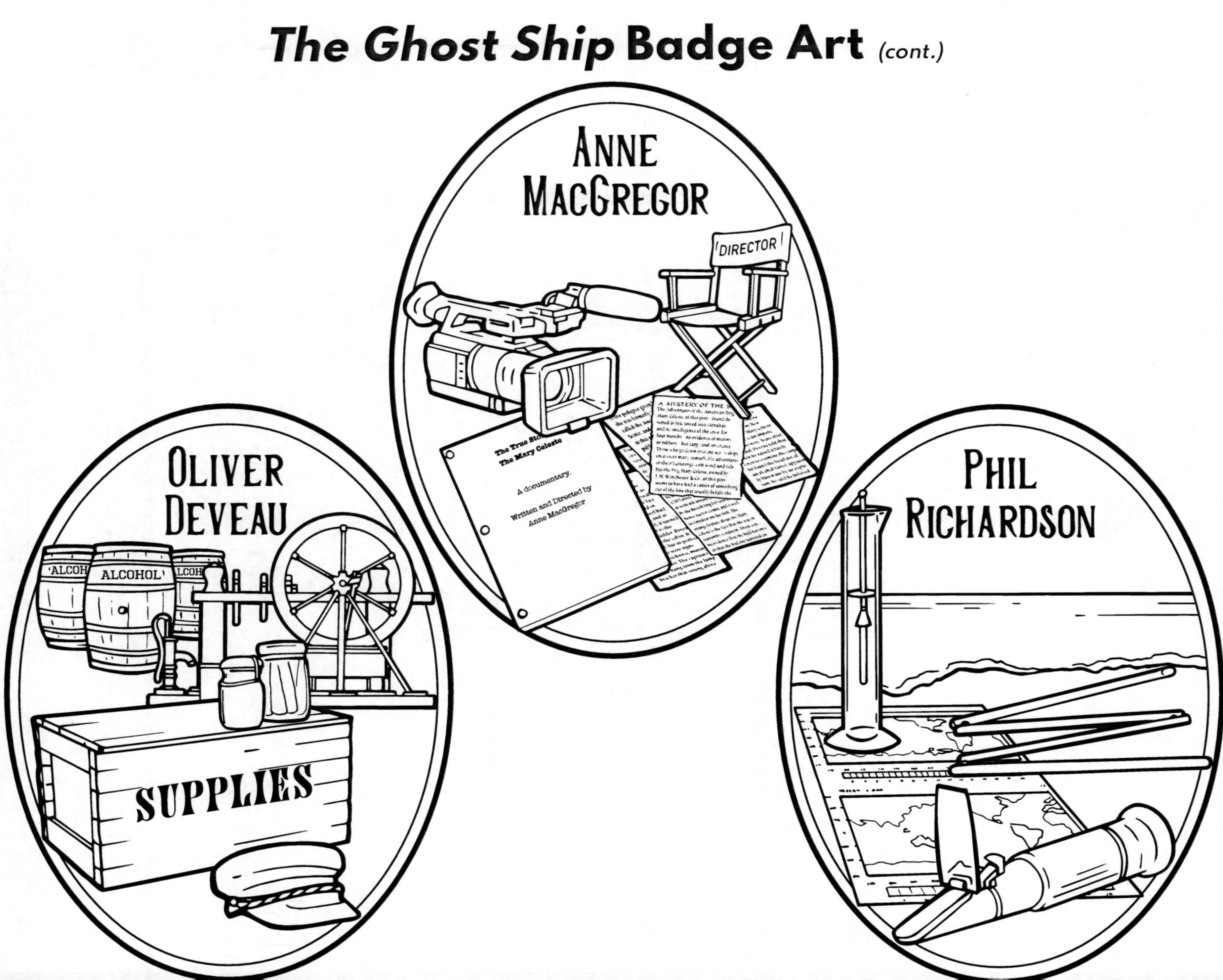

The Ghost Ship Script

Setting

Act 1 takes place on a ship off the coast of Portugal. Act 2 takes place in an oceanography lab.

Characters
- Narrator 1
- Narrator 2
- Captain David Morehouse
- Oliver Deveau
- Anne MacGregor
- Phil Richardson

Act 1

Captain David: It can't be … [*gasps*]. Oliver, do you see what I see?

Oliver: Yes, Captain. It seems to be a ship.

Narrator 1: Captain David is sailing with his crew. They are in the Atlantic Ocean.

Narrator 2: The captain sees something unusual through his spyglass. A spyglass is a tool that sailors use to see far away.

Captain David: That's not just any ship. It looks like the *Mary Celeste*.

Narrator 2: The *Mary Celeste* was thought to be cursed. Over time, it had many captains. Some captains ended up sick. One captain crashed the ship into another ship! That ship sank. Another captain had the ship driven ashore during a storm. It was damaged. Then, while the ship was being fixed, it caught on fire!

Narrator 1: In 1872, a new captain took command. His name was Benjamin Briggs. He was a good sailor. He was known for being fair and kind. His crew liked him.

Oliver: The *Mary Celeste*! Isn't that Captain Briggs' ship?

Captain David: Yes, it is. But I just spoke to Briggs. I had dinner with his family in New York. He set sail a week before we did. Why would his ship be here? He was headed for Italy.

Oliver: Well, Captain, it doesn't look like they made it that far. The ship looks abandoned. The sails are torn. I don't think anyone is steering. What do you want to do?

The Ghost Ship Script *(cont.)*

Captain David: Let's change course. Maybe they need help.

Narrator 1: Captain David and First Mate Oliver told the crew to sail toward the ship. Captain David was worried about Briggs. He wanted to make sure that his friend was okay.

Oliver: I have heard some stories about that ship. It seems to carry bad luck with it wherever it sails.

Narrator 2: Despite the history of bad luck, Captain Briggs was not afraid. He did not believe that the *Mary Celeste* was cursed. He hired a good crew of sailors to join him. He also took his wife and two-year-old daughter on the ship with him.

Captain David: Drop anchor here. Oliver, take a few sailors over to the *Mary Celeste*. I need you to investigate.

Oliver: Aye, aye, Captain!

Narrator 2: First Mate Oliver boarded the *Mary Celeste*. He walked around the silent ship.

Narrator 1: There were no crew members on board. It looked like everyone had vanished! But they left all of their things behind. The ship was stocked with enough food to last for six months.

Narrator 2: Oliver searched the entire ship. One lifeboat was missing. The rooms under the deck were flooded with almost four feet of water.

Narrator 1: Oliver and the other sailors were puzzled. They went back to their ship. They needed to tell Captain David about what they saw.

Captain David: So, what did you find? I keep thinking that it must be pirates.

Narrator 1: Pirates were known to take over ships. They would steal food and supplies.

The Ghost Ship Script (cont.)

Oliver: No, Captain. I thought the same thing. But everything is still on board. The galley is stocked with food. The cabin is full of clothing and supplies.

Captain David: But that doesn't make sense! I know Captain Briggs. He would never abandon his ship. Something terrible must have happened.

Oliver: It is strange. The cabin is flooded. But that's something we can fix.

Captain David: Briggs knows how to fix that, though! The ship looks seaworthy to me. There has to be something else.

Oliver: I took the logbook for you to read. Maybe there are some clues in it.

Narrator 2: Every ship has a logbook. This is a diary for the captain to write down what happens each day.

Captain David: The last entry was November 25. That was nine days ago. There is nothing unusual. Briggs wrote that there was some bad weather. It also says that they had to anchor for two days. But nothing more.

Oliver: I noticed that there were a few tools missing. Plus, the lifeboat is gone. They left in a hurry.

Captain David: We can't just leave the ship here. Let's split the crew. You sail the *Mary Celeste*. You can follow us to shore.

Oliver: I need a few days to fix the rigging. But everything else is in good shape.

Narrator 1: Oliver spent three days fixing the sails and the ropes. Then, he sailed for shore.

Narrator 2: The *Mary Celeste* reached the shore of Gibraltar on Friday the 13th. This is thought to be an unlucky day. Captain David and Oliver turned in the ship. They wanted to get a salvage reward. This is money awarded to people who rescue damaged ships.

The Ghost Ship Script *(cont.)*

Narrator 1: But they were not so lucky. They ended up going to court. People did not believe that Captain Briggs would abandon his ship. They thought Captain David and Oliver stole the ship.

Narrator 2: The judge could not find proof. So, the crew won the trial. But they were only awarded a small sum of money.

Narrator 1: So, what really did happen? In 2002, Anne MacGregor wanted to solve the mystery. She makes documentaries. These are films about real-life events. She met with Phil Richardson. He is an oceanographer. This means that he studies the ocean. Anne needed his help.

Act 2

Anne: Nice to meet you, Phil. Thank you for letting me come to your lab. I have some questions for you.

Phil: Well, I am happy to work on this project with you. I remember reading about the legend of the ghost ship. I would love to finally solve the mystery!

Anne: I studied all the possible theories. They don't make sense. Giant sea monsters? Pirates who didn't steal a thing? One theory said there was a mutiny. But Captain Briggs was loved by his crew. And that doesn't explain where the other crew members went. They wouldn't take control over the ship and then abandon it.

Narrator 2: A mutiny is when sailors refuse to take orders from their captain. Then, they take control of the ship.

Phil: A mutiny is not likely. Captain Briggs had his wife and daughter on board. Plus, he was known for being a great sailor and a fair captain.

Anne: What if something scared them? I read about strange forces of nature. There are earthquakes and tornados in the ocean, right?

The Ghost Ship Script *(cont.)*

Phil: You mean a waterspout? That is possible. But it would have to flood the ship enough to make the captain choose to flee. There were notes about the ship being clean and in order. Also, Briggs took his navigation tools when he left the ship. That means he had enough time to think about what he needed to take with him. A waterspout is unlikely.

Anne: So, it was aliens!

Phil: Ha, ha! Also, a possibility. But not one I will be able to prove.

Anne: The only other theory is that Captain David stole the ship and made Briggs and his crew leave. But I refuse to believe that one. Captain David and Captain Briggs were friends. And Captain David would have to get his whole crew to lie about finding the ship abandoned. I don't think that is possible.

Phil: I agree. I don't think any of those theories make much sense. We need to figure out *why* Captain Briggs would abandon ship. The lifeboat was missing. They must have tried to save themselves from something.

Anne: Agreed. That is why I came to you! I think if we can find the exact spot that they abandoned the ship, we might find more clues. I read the logbook entries from the *Mary Celeste*. On November 25, the ship was six miles from the island of Santa Maria. But when the ship was found ten days later, it was 400 miles east of the island. Is it possible that the ship drifted that far?

Phil: I will investigate. I need to look at the water temperature at that time. I also want to check the wind speed and direction on those days.

Narrator 1: Phil looked at all of the data. He learned that it was possible for the ship to drift that many miles.

Anne: So the *Mary Celeste* really was a ghost ship! It sailed for ten days with no crew.

Phil: There was a rough storm the night before the last log entry.

The Ghost Ship Script *(cont.)*

Anne: But would that be enough of a reason to abandon the ship?

Phil: Maybe not. But the logbook also had his recorded location. He was over 100 miles west from where he *thought* he was. Maybe his navigation tools were broken. He could have panicked if he didn't know where he was.

Anne: That still seems like not enough. It would take a lot for the captain to order everyone to leave the ship.

Phil: You are right. The records say that there was a pump on the ship that was taken apart. Maybe the pump broke and the captain thought the ship might sink?

Anne: Well, they would need to be close enough to shore to get in the lifeboat, right?

Phil: The logbook said they switched course. They were headed north of Santa Maria. Maybe they saw land and decided to leave quickly while the weather was good.

Anne: So Captain Briggs thought his ship might sink. He waited for the storm to end. Then, as soon as he saw land, they took a chance. They jumped in the lifeboat to sail to shore.

Phil: That is my best guess. But nothing can be proven.

Anne: And we still don't know what happened to the lifeboat full of the crew members. They were close enough to make it to shore. It seems like the *Mary Celeste* is still an unsolved mystery. I will continue to research.

Narrator 2: Despite Anne and Phil's research, the case has not been solved. How did a crew vanish off a seaworthy ship? What do *you* think happened?

The Ghost Ship Activity

1. Why did the court think that Captain David and Oliver were lying about how they found the ship?

____

2. Why do you think it was strange that the food and supplies were left behind on the ship?

____

____

3. What is Phil's best guess as to what happened?

____

____

4. Do you think this mystery will ever be solved? Why or why not?

____

____

____

Reader's Theater Reflections

Think about your performance. Color in the number of stars to show how well you did in each area.

Accuracy: I read my part correctly.	☆ ☆ ☆
Rate: I read at a pace that was not too fast or too slow.	☆ ☆ ☆
Expression: I read my character's part with feeling and emotion.	☆ ☆ ☆

List one way that you can improve your reader's theater performance.

____

____

The Ghost Ship

The Ghost Ship Journal

The ghost ship *Mary Celeste* was found in 1872. No one knows what happened to the crew. It remains an unsolved mystery. What do you think happened?

The Lake Monster Lesson Plan

Content Objectives

- Read grade-level text orally with accuracy, appropriate rate, and expression on successive readings.
- Read grade-level text with purpose and understanding.
- Acknowledge differences in the points of view of characters, including by speaking in a different voice for each character when reading dialogue aloud.

Materials

- student copies of *The Lake Monster* Badge Art (pages 64–65)
- student copies of *The Lake Monster* Script (pages 66–71)
- student copies of *The Lake Monster* Activity (page 72)
- student copies of *The Lake Monster* Journal (page 73)
- highlighters, crayons, markers

Before Reading

1. Begin by assessing students' prior knowledge (if any) of the mystery of the lake monster in Lake Champlain. Known as Champ, he is often referred to as the American version of the Loch Ness Monster. (Students may have prior knowledge of Nessie.) Lake Champlain is a large lake between New York and Vermont. There have been reported monster sightings since the 1800s. Most reports are similar and describe a serpent or a dinosaur-looking giant that has humps on its back. Some people say it looks like a giant seahorse that is up to 80 feet long. Some scientists think the descriptions sound like a *plesiosaur*, which was a water reptile that lived during the dinosaur age. Those reptiles lived in saltwater. Although Lake Champlain is a freshwater lake, it was once connected to the Atlantic Ocean. There is a theory that over time, the land rose and cut off the flow of saltwater slowly until the lake became freshwater. Perhaps Champ learned to adapt to the new environment. Scientists have also recorded underwater noises that sound like echolocation used by whales and dolphins. If the sounds are coming from Champ, he might be related to a prehistoric whale or even a long-necked sea turtle. The only thing that is certain is that Champ's existence is still an unsolved mystery, even after decades of investigation.

2. Tell students that they will be performing a reader's theater play about the unsolved mystery of Champ, the legendary lake monster. Distribute copies of the script. Assign students their roles based on reading proficiencies. See page 63 for a list of the reading levels for each role in *The Lake Monster* script.

The Lake Monster **Lesson Plan** *(cont.)*

Rehearsal

1. Once students have been assigned their parts, tell them to go through the entire script and highlight their parts. Then, give students time to silently read either the entire script or just their highlighted sections. Ask them to use a pencil and underline any words that they do not know or do not know how to pronounce. Go over these words together to ensure understanding.

2. This script has key vocabulary that students may not know. Consider creating a word wall. Write the following words from the play on the board or a piece of chart paper: *churning, sturgeon, fossils, emerge, analyzed, expert, data, sonar, zoologist, prehistoric, eyewitness.* Ask students to help you define each one. Write the definitions next to the words. If students are unsure of the definitions, have them read the dictionary definition to you.

3. Give students time to practice their reader's theater. Remind them to speak with fluency, rate, expression, and tone. They need to play the role of the character using just their voices! Demonstrate reading a few lines in a dull, monotonous tone. Then, read the same lines with expression and ask students to explain the difference. Do the same thing with reading pace (read lines too quickly or too slowly) and then demonstrate a proper pace. Lastly, whisper lines softly. Then, read them again with a proper volume. Ask students if they understand the differences.

Performance

1. There are a variety of ways for your students to perform *The Lake Monster* reader's theater. See pages 5–8 for performance ideas.

2. Distribute copies of the badges (pages 64–65). Give students time to decorate their character's badge using crayons or markers.

3. Remind students to speak loudly and clearly and with confidence! Encourage them to show emotion and feeling with their voices. Even the narrators can show emotion by reading their parts with an authoritative and confident tone! If stage fright or public speaking is an issue for some students, remind them to focus on their lines instead of worrying about the audience. And lastly, remind students to take a deep breath, smile, and have fun with this!

Assessment

1. Distribute student copies of *The Lake Monster* Activity (page 72). Go over the activity sheet together and then have students complete it independently.

2. Distribute student copies of *The Lake Monster* Journal (page 73). Remind students that despite the stories of tourists and locals, there still isn't much proof that Champ exists. It is still an unsolved mystery. Discuss the possible theories presented in the script, along with any of your own. Then, give students time to journal their theories.

The Lake Monster Characters

Assigning Characters

The roles in this reader's theater have been leveled to fit the individual needs of your students. When students feel confident in their reading fluency, they will engage with the character and feel comfortable performing in front of others. Remind students that they are performing a play using only their voices. The way they speak each word matters! Demonstrate the difference between monotone reading and reading with fluency and expression so students can understand the expectations.

You might also consider assigning nonspeaking roles to students who are reluctant to read aloud. These students could act as directors or coaches. Remind them that their role is very important. They will have to know the script extremely well and will be in charge of prompting students when it is their turn to read.

The Lake Monster has six roles. They are listed here in order of highest reading-level proficiency to lowest.

Grade 3 Reading Levels:

Narrator 1   Played by: _______________________________

Narrator 2   Played by: _______________________________

Katy Elizabeth Played by: _______________________________

Grade 2/High Grade 1 Reading Levels:

News Reporter Played by: _______________________________

Sandra Mansi Played by: _______________________________

Anthony Mansi Played by: _______________________________

The Lake Monster Badge Art

The Lake Monster Badge Art (cont.)

The Lake Monster Script

The Lake Monster

Setting

Act 1 takes place on the shore of Lake Champlain in 1977. Act 2 takes place 40 years later at Lake Champlain.

Act 1

Sandra: Kids, don't go out too far! I bet the water is freezing.

Narrator 1: Sandra Mansi was on vacation with her family. It was July 5, 1977. She grew up in Vermont. She wanted to show her kids, Heidi and Larry, where she spent her summers as a child.

Narrator 2: Sandra and her husband Anthony sat on the shore and watched the kids wade out into the blue waters of Lake Champlain.

Anthony: It is really beautiful here, Sandi. It's great to see the lake and the places that you visited as a kid. I never thought the lake would be so huge. We should take some pictures. I am going to run back to the car and grab the camera.

Sandra: Okay, Anthony. But be quick. I told the kids we would stop for lunch soon.

Narrator 1: Anthony went back to the car to find their camera. They had a Kodak Instamatic camera.

Narrator 2: This was in the 1970s. There were no cell phones or digital pictures. People took photos on film. They would turn in the film to a photo shop. The shop would use the film to print the photos.

Narrator 1: While Anthony was gone, Sandra stared out at the water. She thought about being a child out on the lake with her grandfather.

Narrator 2: Lake Champlain is a big lake. It is 12 miles wide and 124 miles long. Some places are 400 feet deep.

Characters

- Sandra Mansi
- Anthony Mansi
- Katy Elizabeth
- News Reporter
- Narrator 1
- Narrator 2

The Lake Monster Script *(cont.)*

Narrator 1: As the kids splashed in the lake, Sandra noticed a ripple in the water. It was about 150 feet from the shore.

Sandra: Hey, Heidi and Larry, look at that! It looks like a big school of fish. Do you see the motion in the water?

Narrator 2: But the churning in the water grew bigger.

Sandra: Maybe it's a sturgeon! My grandfather loved to tell us stories about the size of sturgeon.

Narrator 1: Sturgeon are very old fish. They can live to be 150 years old. They are called living fossils because they existed during dinosaur times. That was 120 million years ago!

Narrator 2: Sturgeon can grow very big. Some weigh 300 pounds!

Sandra: Wait a minute— I don't know what that is.

Narrator 1: Sandra saw a head and neck emerge from the water. The creature had a curved back that looked like a hump. She had never seen anything like it.

Anthony: Sandra, what is that? That can't be a fish. It has such a long neck. It looks like a dinosaur. Kids, get out of the water now! I am not sure it is safe here.

Narrator 2: Heidi and Larry got out of the water. Anthony took them back to the car.

Narrator 1: Sandra kept watching the strange-looking creature swim through the lake.

Anthony: The kids are safe in the car. Here, take the camera.

Narrator 2: Sandra was sitting on the ground. As Anthony helped her to her feet, she took one photo with her camera.

Narrator 1: They watched the monster duck under the water.

The Lake Monster Script (cont.)

Anthony: Do you hear that boat in the distance? The noise must have scared it off. What was that thing? Have you seen it before?

Sandra: [*whispering*] I think it was Champ.

Anthony: Who is Champ?

Sandra: My grandfather used to tell us stories about the legend of Champ. He said there was a lake monster that lived here. I never thought it could be true! Maybe there is another explanation for this.

Anthony: Maybe. But I saw it too. That thing was not a fish. Should we tell someone?

Sandra: I don't know if they would believe us.

Narrator 1: The Mansi family left the lake and went out to lunch. They enjoyed the rest of their vacation and returned to their home.

Narrator 2: But then, Sandra had the film developed. When the picture came back, she was amazed. It really did look like a sea serpent swimming in the lake.

Narrator 1: Sandra didn't show anyone the photo for years. But one day she told a friend about it. After that, her story spread quickly. People had been searching for Champ for a long time. All they needed was proof!

Sandra: I agreed to let the *New York Times* publish the photo in 1981. Many people didn't believe me. They think I made it up. But I know what I saw. The photo reminds me of that day.

Narrator 2: Sometimes, people create fake photos of creatures to become famous. But Sandra's photo was analyzed. They proved it was a real photo.

Narrator 1: The photo is real. But is it really a lake monster? Some people think it is a piece of wood floating in the water.

The Lake Monster Script *(cont.)*

Narrator 2: Another problem is that Sandra threw out the negatives. Those are strips of film that the printed photos are made from. Without them, there was only one copy of her photo.

Narrator 1: And Sandra could not provide an exact location for where the sighting took place. She remembers driving down a dirt road on the Vermont side of the lake.

Sandra: I am not an expert. I do not know what Champ is. But I know that I saw it. Plus, my photo was enough proof to make Champ protected by law. New York and Vermont say it is illegal to do any harm to Champ. He is a protected species!

Act 2

Narrator 2: It's been 40 years since Sandra took her famous photo of Champ. And sightings of Champ have continued. Most people see the same shape. They describe the body as being snake-like. It usually has at least one hump and a long neck. It is often seen as being black, green, or gray.

Narrator 1: Katy Elizabeth studies Lake Champlain. She collects data. Today, Katy is meeting with a news reporter to talk about her work. They meet on the shore of the lake.

News Reporter: Hello, Katy. Thank you for agreeing to this interview for the *Vermont Times*. We heard that you have been doing some great work out here on Lake Champlain. Can you tell us about it?

Katy: Thank you for meeting with me. I am the director of a group called "Champ Search." I have been a believer ever since I first saw Champ in 2012. I was camping. I saw a large hump come out of the water. It was not a fish.

News Reporter: That is so interesting! So, what has your group discovered so far?

Katy: We have a boat that we named *Kelpie*. We spend many hours out on the lake. We do lots of research. But on August 5, 2019, we found something really special.

The Lake Monster

The Lake Monster Script *(cont.)*

News Reporter: Was it another Champ sighting?

Katy: Yes, but this one was new. We were scanning the bottom of the lake with our sonar system. We send out radio waves under the water. When the waves hit an object, they bounce back. We can see the fish under the water. We can also take pictures.

News Reporter: Wait! So you took an underwater photo of Champ?

Katy: I saw some strange images at the bottom of the lake. We were sailing across the water fast. I think we were going 45 miles per hour. I took a few screenshots of what was on the sonar screen. The next day I looked at them. One image shows a very large animal. It does not look like a fish. It looks about 25 feet long.

News Reporter: Do you think there is more than one Champ?

Katy: Yes. There have been sightings for over a hundred years. The reports are of animals that range in size. I think most likely there is a group of them. Some sightings say he is a serpent or a snake.

News Reporter: I have read that some zoologists think Champ might be a prehistoric whale or a reptile. Do you think that is possible?

Katy: Anything is possible. I think that nobody really knows for sure. That is why my research is so important. I grew up on this lake. I know what the fish look like. Sturgeon are huge. Some people claim that the lake monster is just a sturgeon. But Champ doesn't look like a fish. Others say it is a piece of floating wood or a large neck of a bird on the water. But there are so many eyewitnesses. Often Champ is spotted by multiple people at the same time. They all agree that it is unlike any creature they have seen. It seems hard not to believe in Champ.

News Reporter: Although, sometimes seeing is believing. I am not sure I am convinced.

The Lake Monster Script *(cont.)*

Katy: I understand. I grew up here, so the legend of Champ was always a real possibility to me. I work hard to make sure Champ and creatures like him are protected. I convinced the town of Port Henry to pass a law that protects Champ.

News Reporter: You even wrote a book about Champ. Tell us about that.

Katy: Yes, I wrote a book called *The Water Horse of Lake Champlain.* It gives the reader a history of the lake. It lists the many sightings. It also has research on Champ. Scientists recorded sounds coming from the lake. They thought it was from a whale or dolphin. But we know that those animals do not live in the freshwater of Lake Champlain. Those sounds are still a mystery.

News Reporter: I think that sounds like a great book for anyone interested in learning more about—[*gasps*]

Narrator 1: The news reporter stops speaking. She looks out at the churning waters of Lake Champlain.

Narrator 2: A curved neck bobs out of the water once. Then, it disappears under the surface.

News Reporter: Did you see that?! I think it was Champ!

Katy: I didn't see it. But you might have just had your first sighting.

News Reporter: I guess it could have been a tree branch. But— it really looked like a cute, dinosaur-looking snake.

Katy: Ha, ha! That sounds like Champ.

Narrator 1: The mystery of the lake monster remains unsolved. There are countless scientists and researchers trying to solve it.

Narrator 2: The Champ sightings continue every year.

Narrator 1: Is there really a lake monster swimming in Lake Champlain?

Narrator 2: Or is there another explanation? What do *you* think?

The Lake Monster Activity

1. Why did some people think Sandra's photo was fake?

____

____

2. It is possible that Champ is not a monster. List something people could be seeing that might appear to be a monster.

____

3. What do you think the news reporter means by saying "seeing is believing"?

____

____

4. Do you think this mystery will ever be solved? Why or why not?

____

____

____

Reader's Theater Reflections

Think about your performance. Color in the number of stars to show how well you did in each area.

Accuracy: I read my part correctly.	☆ ☆ ☆
Rate: I read at a pace that was not too fast or too slow.	☆ ☆ ☆
Expression: I read my character's part with feeling and emotion.	☆ ☆ ☆

List one way that you can improve your reader's theater performance.

____

____

The Lake Monster Journal

The legend of Champ, the lake monster, has been around for years. There are many stories about Champ. But there is little evidence. Do you believe that Champ exists? Explain why or why not.

The Lost Colony Lesson Plan

Content Objectives

- Read grade-level text orally with accuracy, appropriate rate, and expression on successive readings.
- Read grade-level text with purpose and understanding.
- Acknowledge differences in the points of view of characters, including by speaking in a different voice for each character when reading dialogue aloud.

Materials

- student copies of *The Lost Colony* Badge Art (pages 77–78)
- student copies of *The Lost Colony* Script (pages 79–84)
- student copies of *The Lost Colony* Activity (page 85)
- student copies of *The Lost Colony* Journal (page 86)
- highlighters, crayons, markers

Before Reading

1. Begin by assessing students' prior knowledge (if any) of the lost colony of Roanoke. Give students some background information about the colony. In 1584, a large piece of American land was granted to Sir Walter Raleigh in England. It was given to him by Queen Elizabeth I (even though it technically was not her land to give). Sir Walter wanted to create English colonies in the New World. The colonies would be towns or settlements full of English colonists who were still under the rule of the Queen. The first trip to Roanoke Island (off the coast of modern-day North Carolina) was in 1585. The settlers were all men (mostly soldiers). They set up a fort on the island. But they battled with the Native Americans who already lived there. Most of the men returned to England, including a man named John White. A small group of colonists stayed behind. In 1587, John White led a new group of 115 colonists. That group included his daughter Eleanor and her husband. When they arrived on the island, they found a human skeleton. The rest of the men were gone. This new group set out to build a better settlement. But with winter approaching, they did not have enough food. White went back to England for more food and supplies. But his trip was delayed. It took him nearly three years to return. When he finally returned to Roanoke, the entire colony of over a hundred colonists was abandoned. It looked like they vanished. There are many theories, but to this day, it remains an unsolved mystery.

2. Tell students that they will be performing a reader's theater play about the unsolved mystery of the lost colony of Roanoke. Distribute copies of the script. Assign students their roles based on reading proficiencies. See page 76 for a list of the reading levels for each role in *The Lost Colony* script.

The Lost Colony **Lesson Plan** *(cont.)*

Rehearsal

1. Once students have been assigned their parts, tell them to go through the entire script and highlight their parts. Then, give students time to silently read either the entire script or just their highlighted sections. Ask them to use a pencil and underline any words that they do not know or do not know how to pronounce. Go over these words together to ensure understanding.

2. This script has key vocabulary that students may not know. Have students write down the following words from the play on a piece of paper: *colony, colonist, archeologist, ancestry, inherited, erosion, artifacts, canteen.* Have students look up the definition of each and then draw a picture to match each word.

3. Give students time to practice their reader's theater. Remind them to speak with fluency, rate, expression, and tone. They need to play the role of the character using just their voices! Demonstrate reading a few lines in a dull, monotonous tone. Then, read the same lines with expression and ask students to explain the difference. Do the same thing with reading pace (read lines too quickly or too slowly) and then demonstrate a proper pace. Lastly, whisper lines softly. Then, read them again with a proper volume. Ask students if they understand the differences.

Performance

1. There are a variety of ways for your students to perform *The Lost Colony* reader's theater. See pages 5–8 for performance ideas.

2. Distribute copies of the badges (pages 77–78). Give students time to decorate their character's badge using crayons or markers.

3. Remind students to speak loudly and clearly and with confidence! Encourage them to show emotion and feeling with their voices. Even the narrators can show emotion by reading their parts with an authoritative and confident tone! If stage fright or public speaking is an issue for some students, remind them to focus on their lines instead of worrying about the audience. And lastly, remind students to take a deep breath, smile, and have fun with this!

Assessment

1. Distribute student copies of *The Lost Colony* Activity (page 85). Go over the activity sheet together and then have students complete it independently.

2. Distribute student copies of *The Lost Colony* Journal (page 86). Remind students that despite the many theories presented over the years, no one is certain of what really happened to the colonists. It is still an unsolved mystery. Discuss the possible theories presented in the script, along with any of your own. Then, give students time to journal their theories.

The Lost Colony Characters

Assigning Characters

The roles in this reader's theater have been leveled to fit the individual needs of your students. When students feel confident in their reading fluency, they will engage with the character and feel comfortable performing in front of others. Remind students that they are performing a play using only their voices. The way they speak each word matters! Demonstrate the difference between monotone reading and reading with fluency and expression so students can understand the expectations.

You might also consider assigning nonspeaking roles to students who are reluctant to read aloud. These students could act as directors or coaches. Remind them that their role is very important. They will have to know the script extremely well and will be in charge of prompting students when it is their turn to read.

The Lost Colony has six roles. They are listed here in order of highest reading-level proficiency to lowest.

Grade 3 Reading Levels:

Narrator 1   Played by: ______________________________

Narrator 2   Played by: ______________________________

Archeologist Walsh Played by: ______________________________

Grade 2/High Grade 1 Reading Levels:

Archeologist Greene Played by: ______________________________

John White   Played by: ______________________________

Eleanor Dare   Played by: ______________________________

The Lost Colony Badge Art

The Lost Colony Badge Art (cont.)

The Lost Colony Script

Characters
- Narrator 1
- Narrator 2
- John White
- Eleanor Dare
- Archeologist Walsh
- Archeologist Greene

Setting

Act 1 takes place on Roanoke Island, off the coast of North Carolina. Act 2 takes place at the Fort Raleigh National Historic site. This is the modern-day location of the lost colony.

Act 1

Narrator 1: The year is 1587. An English ship is sailing to America. The ship has over a hundred people on board.

Narrator 2: The Queen of England sent these people to America. They are called colonists. These colonists would be living on American land. But they would still be under her rule.

Narrator 1: The ship sailed to Roanoke Island. It is near the coast of North Carolina.

Narrator 2: The group is led by John White. He is to be the governor of the new colony. This was his second trip to the island. He sailed to Roanoke two years earlier.

Narrator 1: The first group built a fort. They struggled to stay alive. The weather was stormy. They fought with the local Native American tribes. Many of the colonists went back to England. John was one of them.

Narrator 2: But John wanted to try again. He had big dreams of starting a colony that would last forever.

Narrator 1: England was at war with Spain. Colonists came to America hoping for a better life. They wanted more freedom and safety.

Narrator 2: John's daughter Eleanor and her husband joined him on the second trip. Eleanor wanted to start a new life in America.

The Lost Colony Script *(cont.)*

John: Well, Eleanor, welcome to the New World! What do you think?

Eleanor: Father, it looks just like your paintings! There are so many pine trees. It's beautiful. And it is very quiet. I imagine life here will be much different than it was back in England.

John: It is very quiet. We left fifteen people behind. I wonder where they went. The fort looks abandoned.

Eleanor: Maybe they moved to a new spot? Or maybe a ship came and they returned to England?

John: That is possible. It looks like they left things in need of repair. We have much work to do. We can start by fixing the old buildings. Then, we can build new homes. And we need to grow food to eat. Starting a colony that lasts is going to be a challenge.

Eleanor: I have hope for our future here in this New World. I want my children to live far away from the war. It is peaceful here. Let's get to work!

Narrator 1: The group began fixing the buildings. And they started building their own homes. While digging, they found something strange.

Eleanor: [*gasps*] Father, look at this! It looks like a skeleton.

John: Oh, no! That is a human skeleton. It could be one of the settlers that stayed behind. I was hoping they had moved on. But it looks like they didn't survive. I wonder what happened. Maybe they ran out of supplies.

Eleanor: But we have more supplies this time, right? We can make it work.

John: I think so, dear.

Narrator 2: The colonists worked hard during the summer months. And on August 18, they had a big celebration.

Narrator 1: Eleanor gave birth to a baby girl.

The Lost Colony Script (cont.)

Eleanor: Father, I would like you to meet your granddaughter. Her name is Virginia.

John: Oh, Eleanor. She is perfect. Welcome to the world, Virginia Dare. You are the first English baby born in the New World!

Narrator 2: But John began to worry about the future. They were running out of supplies. They hadn't grown as much food as he hoped. The winter would be freezing. He worried about his daughter and his new baby granddaughter.

Narrator 1: The colonists took a vote. They wanted John to return to England for supplies.

John: I am hesitant to leave you all behind. It may be months before my return.

Eleanor: Don't worry, father. We will all be fine. Stay safe in your travels. We will be together again soon.

John: We need a plan. If you are forced to leave, carve a symbol in the big tree.

Eleanor: That is a great idea. I will carve a symbol of a cross. This will tell you if we are in danger or were attacked. And if we choose to leave, we will carve a message for you. It will tell you where we went. When you get back, you will be able to find us. But don't worry too much, Father. We have been safe here so far. We will be waiting for your speedy return.

John: Farewell, Roanoke colony! I will return soon. It will only be a few months.

Narrator 1: But John White did not return soon. His voyage home was difficult. He arrived in England during the war. Every ship in England was being used for battle. He had no way to communicate with the colonists in the New World.

Narrator 2: It took two years, but White finally found a ship. He filled it with supplies to take back to Roanoke. He weathered many terrible storms and battles at sea. But he finally returned to Roanoke Island.

The Lost Colony Script *(cont.)*

Narrator 1: It was August 18, 1590. It was Virginia Dare's third birthday. John stepped on the familiar shores of Roanoke. He was waiting to be met by his daughter and granddaughter. But he found a quiet and empty island. It was abandoned.

John: Eleanor? Virginia? Where have you gone?

Narrator 2: John searched the colony for clues. He only found one.

Narrator 1: There was a carving in the tree. It was not a cross. It was the letters "CRO." There was also a carving in the fence. It read, "CROATOAN."

John: This is good news! There is no cross. That means they chose to leave on their own. There was no danger. Croatoan is an island close to here. The Croatoan tribe is living there. I hope they let them stay.

Narrator 2: John returned to his ship. But the captain would not sail to Croatoan. Another storm was coming. With a sad heart, John went back to England. He never had a chance to return.

Act 2

Narrator 1: The mystery of the lost colony was never solved. But the search still continues.

Narrator 2: In 2009, scientists had a research dig. It was at the Fort Raleigh National Historic Site. This is the present-day location of Roanoke Island.

Narrator 1: Archeologists worked together. They looked for artifacts buried under the ground. They were hoping to find clues that solved the mystery of the lost colony.

Walsh: Today's the last day of digging. I never thought we would find so many things. It's hard to believe that the entire colony is underground today. Some of it is under the ocean!

The Lost Colony Script *(cont.)*

Greene: Erosion hides the past from us. And that is why we dig! We get to hunt for clues. Although no matter how many artifacts we find, I still have so many questions.

Walsh: I think we have learned so much. We found a mix of items belonging to the settlers and to the Native Americans. There are Native American pots and beads. But there are also English canteens and plates.

Greene: What do you think happened? Do you think the Croatoan tribe took them in?

Walsh: I don't think they were attacked. And I don't think something bad happened. When John White came back, there wasn't a cross carved in the tree. Eleanor would have carved that if they were in danger. White said that the houses were taken down. Nothing looked destroyed. There were no signs of a battle.

Greene: True. Plus, there were over a hundred colonists. If they had died on Roanoke, he would have seen their remains.

Walsh: So, let's say they did go to Croatoan. That island is 50 miles away from here. How do you think they got there?

Greene: I am not sure. I know archeologists found English bowls when they did a research dig there. That is proof that there were some colonists there.

Walsh: The Croatoan tribe was known for being peaceful. I think they found the colonists and knew they needed help. White left because they were running out of food. The best chance for their survival would be to live with the Native Americans. But could the Croatoans take care of a hundred colonists?

Greene: It is possible that they split into smaller groups. Maybe different tribes each took a small group of settlers to live with them.

The Lost Colony Script *(cont.)*

Walsh: That is a good theory too. I think the bigger mystery is why did they leave at all? They could have traded items with the Native Americans for food.

Greene: Maybe Spanish ships came and they were afraid? Spain and England were still at war at the time.

Walsh: That sounds likely. I am certain they survived. I was doing research on another colony called Jamestown. The settlers there heard stories about the Roanoke colonists from the Native Americans.

Greene: I read a report from long ago that said some Native American tribes had built English-style homes. They even had stone walls. The colonists could have taught them how to build these.

Walsh: I have a friend who is a scientist. They are trying to study the DNA of the Native Americans still living on the island. Maybe they can trace their ancestry back. They think that the English colonists joined the Croatoan tribe. There are stories of Native Americans with gray eyes and blonde hair. They could have inherited those traits from the colonists.

Greene: So maybe they were never really a lost colony. I think they were saved by the Croatoan tribe and joined their people. Over time, they blended their two groups into one.

Walsh: The Roanoke colony is still a mystery. But I like your theory the most. It beats being captured by aliens.

Greene: Or being eaten by zombies!

Narrator 1: There are many theories about what happened to the lost colony of Roanoke.

Narrator 2: Despite modern tools and research, there is no true proof. It remains an unsolved mystery. What do *you* think happened?

The Lost Colony Activity

1. Why did English colonists want to come to the New World?

____

____

2. Why was building a new colony difficult to do?

____

____

3. What is Archeologist Greene's theory about what happened?

____

____

4. Do you think this mystery will ever be solved? Why or why not?

____

____

____

Reader's Theater Reflections

Think about your performance. Color in the number of stars to show how well you did in each area.

Accuracy: I read my part correctly.	☆ ☆ ☆
Rate: I read at a pace that was not too fast or too slow.	☆ ☆ ☆
Expression: I read my character's part with feeling and emotion.	☆ ☆ ☆

List one way that you can improve your reader's theater performance.

____

The Lost Colony Journal

Research continues at the site of the lost colony. There are many theories about what happened to the missing colonists. What do you think happened?

It's Raining Goo Lesson Plan

Content Objectives

- Read grade-level text orally with accuracy, appropriate rate, and expression on successive readings.
- Read grade-level text with purpose and understanding.
- Acknowledge differences in the points of view of characters, including by speaking in a different voice for each character when reading dialogue aloud.

Materials

- student copies of *It's Raining Goo* Badge Art (pages 90–91)
- student copies of *It's Raining Goo* Script (pages 92–97)
- student copies of *It's Raining Goo* Activity (page 98)
- student copies of *It's Raining Goo* Journal (page 99)
- highlighters, crayons, markers

Before Reading

1. Begin by assessing students' prior knowledge (if any) of strange weather anomalies. Strong winds or tornadoes have caused fish, frogs, and even a dozen golf balls to get sucked up into the sky and then rained back down onto the ground. But one unsolved mystery occurred in a small town in Washington in 1994. The sky rained down tiny blobs of goo all over the town. Nobody knew what the goo was. But many people in the town felt sick after coming in contact with the goo. They were dizzy and sick to their stomachs. Was it because of the goo? Scientists tested samples of the goo, but the results did not determine a definite answer. There are many theories about what happened, including aliens, military experiments, and blown-up bits of jellyfish! The U.S. Air Force was flying planes overhead for practice runs over the Pacific Ocean. But the military denies knowing anything about the goo that fell from the sky. It remains an unsolved mystery to this day.

2. Tell students that they will be performing a reader's theater play about the unsolved mystery of the raining goo. Distribute copies of the script. Assign students their roles based on reading proficiencies. See page 89 for a list of the reading levels for each role in the *It's Raining Goo* script.

It's Raining Goo Lesson Plan *(cont.)*

Rehearsal

1. Once students have been assigned their parts, tell them to go through the entire script and highlight their parts. Then, give students time to silently read either the entire script or just their highlighted sections. Ask them to use a pencil and underline any words that they do not know or do not know how to pronounce. Go over these words together to ensure understanding.

2. This script has key vocabulary that students may not know. Have students write down the following words from the play on a piece of paper: *diagnosis, symptoms, bacteria, virus, experiment, microbiologist, particles, nucleus, fungus.* Have students look up the definitions of the words and then quiz one another on their definitions.

3. Give students time to practice their reader's theater. Remind them to speak with fluency, rate, expression, and tone. They need to play the role of the character using just their voices! Demonstrate reading a few lines in a dull, monotonous tone. Then, read the same lines with expression and ask students to explain the difference. Do the same thing with reading pace (read lines too quickly or too slowly) and then demonstrate a proper pace. Lastly, whisper lines softly. Then, read them again with a proper volume. Ask students if they understand the differences.

Performance

1. There are a variety of ways for your students to perform the *It's Raining Goo* reader's theater. See pages 5–8 for performance ideas.

2. Distribute copies of the badges (pages 90–91). Give students time to decorate their character's badge using crayons or markers.

3. Remind students to speak loudly and clearly and with confidence! Encourage them to show emotion and feeling with their voices. Even the narrators can show emotion by reading their parts with an authoritative and confident tone! If stage fright or public speaking is an issue for some students, remind them to focus on their lines instead of worrying about the audience. And lastly, remind students to take a deep breath, smile, and have fun with this!

Assessment

1. Distribute student copies of the *It's Raining Goo* Activity (page 98). Go over the activity sheet together and then have students complete it independently.

2. Distribute student copies of the *It's Raining Goo* Journal (page 99). Remind students that despite the stories of the residents in Oakville, the origin of the goo was never determined. It is still an unsolved mystery. Discuss the possible theories presented in the script, along with any of your own. Then, give students time to journal their theories.

It's Raining Goo Characters

Assigning Characters

The roles in this reader's theater have been leveled to fit the individual needs of your students. When students feel confident in their reading fluency, they will engage with the character and feel comfortable performing in front of others. Remind students that they are performing a play using only their voices. The way they speak each word matters! Demonstrate the difference between monotone reading and reading with fluency and expression so students can understand the expectations.

You might also consider assigning nonspeaking roles to students who are reluctant to read aloud. These students could act as directors or coaches. Remind them that their role is very important. They will have to know the script extremely well and will be in charge of prompting students when it is their turn to read.

It's Raining Goo has six roles. They are listed here in order of highest reading-level proficiency to lowest.

Grade 3 Reading Levels:

Narrator 2   Played by: _______________________________________

Narrator 1   Played by: _______________________________________

Tim Davis   Played by: _______________________________________

Grade 2/High Grade 1 Reading Levels:

Sunny Barclift   Played by: ___________________________________

Dotty Hearn   Played by: ______________________________________

Officer David Lacey   Played by: ______________________________________

It's Raining Goo Badge Art

It's Raining Goo Badge Art (cont.)

It's Raining Goo Script

Characters
- Narrator 1
- Narrator 2
- Officer David Lacey
- Dotty Hearn
- Sunny Barclift
- Tim Davis

Setting

Act 1 takes place on a rainy day in Oakville, Washington in 1994. Act 2 takes place a year later in a research lab.

Act 1

Narrator 1: It started off like any other day. Even though it was summer, the sky opened up, and rain began falling.

Narrator 2: This was not unusual. Oakville, Washington, is a small town. It is in the northwest part of the United States. It gets a lot of rain. Nobody was surprised when it started to rain. It was August 7, 1994.

Narrator 1: Officer David Lacey was driving down the street in his police car. It was very early in the morning.

Narrator 2: It started to rain hard.

Officer David: [*sigh*] Another rainy summer day here in Oakville. It seems like the rain never stops.

Narrator 1: Officer David turned on his windshield wipers.

Officer David: What in the world? My wipers are smearing the rain. Wait a second. That's not rain. It looks like jelly. I can't see through my windshield!

Narrator 2: Officer David pulled over to the side of the road. He got out to investigate.

Narrator 1: The windshield wipers had smeared the goo across the windshield in a thick paste.

It's Raining Goo Script *(cont.)*

Officer David: Something strange is going on here. I am going to put on some gloves to be safe. I have never seen anything like this before! This rain is squishy. It feels like jelly. These little balls of goo are tiny. They are like gooey pieces of rice. But they don't smell like anything. They clump together and ooze like slime.

Narrator 1: Officer David cleaned off the windshield of his police car. When his work shift ended, he went home. Within a few hours, he felt sick.

Officer David: I was having trouble breathing. I felt sick to my stomach. I was dizzy, and I had a fever. I went straight to bed. I didn't think it had anything to do with the goo. I thought I had the flu. But the strange thing was that I wasn't the only one feeling this way.

Narrator 2: Later that same day, Dotty Hearn woke up. She lived down the road. The goo storm was already over. Dotty didn't see the goo fall from the sky. She thought it was just a regular rainy morning in Oakville. But, when Dotty went outside, she was amazed. Her farm was covered in goo.

Dotty: What kind of storm was that? This looks like hail! But it's not melting. How strange. These aren't pieces of ice. These look like little balls of clear jelly.

Narrator 1: Dotty went back inside her house. Within an hour, she felt sick too.

Dotty: Oh my! I feel terrible. I am so dizzy. I need to lie down.

Narrator 2: Dotty's daughter Sunny found her mother lying on the floor.

Sunny: I knew something was wrong. My mom was cold and sweaty. She said her vision was blurry. Her stomach was upset. She couldn't make the dizzy feeling stop. I took her to the hospital!

Dotty: I was in the hospital for three days! The doctor told me it was an inner ear infection. I thought it was a strange diagnosis. I don't remember ever having those symptoms before with an ear infection.

It's Raining Goo Script *(cont.)*

Sunny: I did not think the doctor was right. I took a sample of the goo to the hospital. I wasn't sure it was related to my mom's sickness. But I thought it was worth finding out. Plus, I heard stories from other neighbors who were also feeling sick after touching the goo.

Narrator 1: The hospital studied a sample of the goo. They found out that it had human white blood cells.

Sunny: The hospital sent the sample to the department of health. They thought that it might be human waste that had fallen from an airplane toilet.

Narrator 2: But, the Federal Aviation Administration said no way. They have rules against planes dumping human waste.

Narrator 1: Plus, they dye all waste a bright blue color. The balls of goo were clear. If human waste ever leaks from a plane, it would freeze. It would not turn to goo.

Sunny: The goo landed on an area of more than 20 square miles. Our entire town was covered in the goo. It didn't make sense for it to come from one plane flying over us.

Officer David: And it rained goo six more times over the next month. After hearing other stories about the goo, I think it is what made me sick that day. My symptoms were similar to Dotty's symptoms. I went to the doctor. They said I had a virus. They were not concerned because I was feeling better. But why was everyone getting sick at the same time? It seemed like our whole town was feeling dizzy and ill. Something wasn't right. It was a mystery. The pieces of goo were small. But when they fell, they clumped together into larger balls of jelly. Thankfully, I did not get sick again.

Narrator 2: A scientist at the department of health also found bacteria in the goo. The bacteria could have come from soil or water. His best guess was there was a virus or bacteria. It was trapped inside of the goo. He also believed the goo was manmade.

It's Raining Goo Script *(cont.)*

Sunny: I called the department of health to learn more about the test results. The scientist who was working on the sample told me something interesting. He said the sample was taken from his lab. When he asked where it went, he was told not to mention the goo again.

Narrator 1: Was the sample lost? Did someone steal it? Was it just misplaced? The mystery continued.

Act 2

Sunny: It seemed like we were never going to get answers. My mom kept a sample of the goo in her freezer. A year later, we decided to go to a private lab.

Dotty: We took the sample to Tim Davis. He is a microbiologist.

Narrator 2: A microbiologist is a scientist. They study tiny life forms.

Narrator 1: They use a microscope to look at animals that are too small to see with our eyes.

Tim: I was surprised when I heard the story behind the goo. I told Dotty and Sunny that I would take a look at the sample. I wasn't sure I could help. But I was surprised when I studied the goo under the microscope.

Dotty: The suspense! What do you think it is?

Tim: I am not sure what it is. But I can tell you this. It is... alive!

Sunny: Alive! Do you think these blobs are animals?

Tim: Not exactly. But they do contain special cells. These cells have a nucleus. These cells come from living creatures. It could be from a plant, animal, or even a fungus. My best guess is this came from something that was at one time alive.

Dotty: So instead of it's raining cats and dogs...

It's Raining Goo Script *(cont.)*

It's Raining Goo

Tim: It's raining… jellyfish?

Sunny: Jellyfish? How is that possible?

Tim: Strange things have fallen from the sky before. All it takes is for something to happen to cause the jellyfish to get trapped in the sky. Then, they eventually fall back down. I have to say, I am not sure this goo is jellyfish particles. I really don't know what it is.

Dotty: There have been a lot of military planes flying overhead. I think they do tests over the ocean.

Sunny: You are right. The Navy does a lot of tests here. Maybe they know something about this.

Narrator 1: The Air Force admitted to conducting practice bombs over the Pacific Ocean. But they deny knowing anything about the raining goo.

Tim: I suppose it's possible that the bombings exploded a school of jellyfish. The pieces of jellyfish could get trapped in the clouds. Then, they rained down.

Sunny: Well, I do not believe that for one second. The Pacific Ocean is 50 miles away.

Tim: I agree that it isn't likely. Plus, you said that the goo rained down six more times. And it only rained down on the town of Oakville. The chances of that randomly happening are very slim.

Dotty: Yeah, I don't believe that theory either. You think if pieces of jellyfish were trapped in the sky, they would start to stink! The goo did not smell like anything. And it made me sick. Why would pieces of jellyfish cause illness?

Tim: Something's fishy. And it's probably not the goo. You said that the military planes were flying overhead? Could it be something they dropped from their planes?

Sunny: Like a military experiment? That could be possible.

It's Raining Goo Script *(cont.)*

Dotty: I live on a farm. I have never seen anything like this goo. I don't think it happened naturally. My theory is someone made the goo. And someone dropped the goo from the sky.

Tim: Another theory is that the illness is not linked to the goo. Oakville is a small town. You may have just been hit with a really bad virus that made its way through the population.

Sunny: So it could just be a coincidence that the people who touched the goo got sick soon after?

Tim: I mean, it is just a theory. Right now, not one theory looks completely correct. Nothing quite adds up. I am not sure this mystery will ever be solved.

Dotty: Our neighbor thinks it's alien goo from outer space.

Tim: Hey, I wouldn't rule that out either!

Sunny: Thank you for your help, Tim. I wonder if this mystery will ever be solved.

Tim: If it ever happens again, bring me another sample. This mysterious goo is a puzzle I want to solve!

Narrator 1: The goo only rained across Oakville in 1994. It has not happened again.

Narrator 2: Was the goo really jellyfish or a military test? Did it come from aliens in outer space? Was it just a prank?

Narrator 1: This is still an unsolved mystery. What do *you* think happened?

It's Raining Goo Activity

1. Why were the people of Oakville worried about the goo?

____

____

2. What is one explanation for how jellyfish could fall from the sky?

____

____

3. Why did Dotty think it wasn't jellyfish?

____

____

4. Do you think this mystery will ever be solved? Why or why not?

____

____

____

Reader's Theater Reflections

Think about your performance. Color in the number of stars to show how well you did in each area.

Accuracy: I read my part correctly.	☆ ☆ ☆
Rate: I read at a pace that was not too fast or too slow.	☆ ☆ ☆
Expression: I read my character's part with feeling and emotion.	☆ ☆ ☆

List one way that you can improve your reader's theater performance.

____

____

It's Raining Goo Journal

The month of rainy goo remains an unsolved mystery. There are many theories about what happened. But no real proof. What do you think happened?

The Stolen Art Lesson Plan

Content Objectives

- Read grade-level text orally with accuracy, appropriate rate, and expression on successive readings.
- Read grade-level text with purpose and understanding.
- Acknowledge differences in the points of view of characters, including by speaking in a different voice for each character when reading dialogue aloud.

Materials

- student copies of *The Stolen Art* Badge Art (pages 103–104)
- student copies of *The Stolen Art* Script (pages 105–110)
- student copies of *The Stolen Art* Activity (page 111)
- student copies of *The Stolen Art* Journal (page 112)
- highlighters, crayons, markers

Before Reading

1. Begin by assessing students' prior knowledge (if any) of the famous art heist in Boston in 1990. Provide some background information on the Isabella Stewart Gardner Museum. Isabella lived from 1840–1924. She received a large inheritance from her father and chose to collect famous works of art. In 1903, she opened her museum to the public. The gallery includes artwork by Titian, Rembrandt, Michelangelo, Raphael, Botticelli, Manet, and Degas. Unfortunately, 13 famous works of art were stolen on March 18, 1990. The FBI has been investigating ever since. It took years for them to determine the identity of the robbers. By that time, both robbers had already died. The unsolved mystery is, where are the stolen pieces of art? Not one has been found. The $10 million reward money is still available to anyone who can safely return the missing paintings.

2. Tell students that they will be performing a reader's theater play about the unsolved mystery of the famous Boston art heist. Distribute copies of the script. Assign students their roles based on reading proficiencies. See page 102 for a list of the reading levels for each role in *The Stolen Art* script.

The Stolen Art Lesson Plan *(cont.)*

Rehearsal

1. Once students have been assigned their parts, tell them to go through the entire script and highlight their parts. Then, give students time to silently read either the entire script or just their highlighted sections. Ask them to use a pencil and underline any words that they do not know or do not know how to pronounce. Go over these words together to ensure understanding.

2. This script has key vocabulary that students may not know. Have students write down the following words from the play on a piece of paper: *commotion, museum, control panel, motion detectors, gallery, bargain.* Have students look up the definition and draw a picture of each word.

3. Give students time to practice their reader's theater. Remind them to speak with fluency, rate, expression, and tone. They need to play the role of the character using just their voices! Demonstrate reading a few lines in a dull, monotonous tone. Then, read the same lines with expression and ask students to explain the difference. Do the same thing with reading pace (read lines too quickly or too slowly) and then demonstrate a proper pace. Lastly, whisper lines softly. Then, read them again with a proper volume. Ask students if they understand the differences.

Performance

1. There are a variety of ways for your students to perform *The Stolen Art* reader's theater. See pages 5–8 for performance ideas.

2. Distribute copies of the badges (pages 103–104). Give students time to decorate their character's badge using crayons or markers.

3. Remind students to speak loudly and clearly and with confidence! Encourage them to show emotion and feeling with their voices. Even the narrators can show emotion by reading their parts with an authoritative and confident tone! If stage fright or public speaking is an issue for some students, remind them to focus on their lines instead of worrying about the audience. And lastly, remind students to take a deep breath, smile, and have fun with this!

Assessment

1. Distribute student copies of *The Stolen Art* Activity (page 111). Go over the activity sheet together and then have students complete it independently.

2. Distribute student copies of *The Stolen Art* Journal (page 112). Remind students that even though the FBI thinks they know who stole the art, the artwork itself is still missing. It is still an unsolved mystery. Discuss the possible theories presented in the script, along with any of your own. Then, give students time to journal their theories.

The Stolen Art Characters

Assigning Characters

The roles in this reader's theater have been leveled to fit the individual needs of your students. When students feel confident in their reading fluency, they will engage with the character and feel comfortable performing in front of others. Remind students that they are performing a play using only their voices. The way they speak each word matters! Demonstrate the difference between monotone reading and reading with fluency and expression so students can understand the expectations.

You might also consider assigning nonspeaking roles to students who are reluctant to read aloud. These students could act as directors or coaches. Remind them that their role is very important. They will have to know the script extremely well and will be in charge of prompting students when it is their turn to read.

The Stolen Art has six roles. They are listed here in order of highest reading-level proficiency to lowest.

Grade 3 Reading Levels:

Narrator Played by: _______________________

Museum Director Anne Hawley Played by: _______________________

Police Officer Wright Played by: _______________________

Grade 2/High Grade 1 Reading Levels:

Police Officer Jones Played by: _______________________

Security Guard Rick Abath Played by: _______________________

Security Guard Randy Hestand Played by: _______________________

The Stolen Art Badge Art

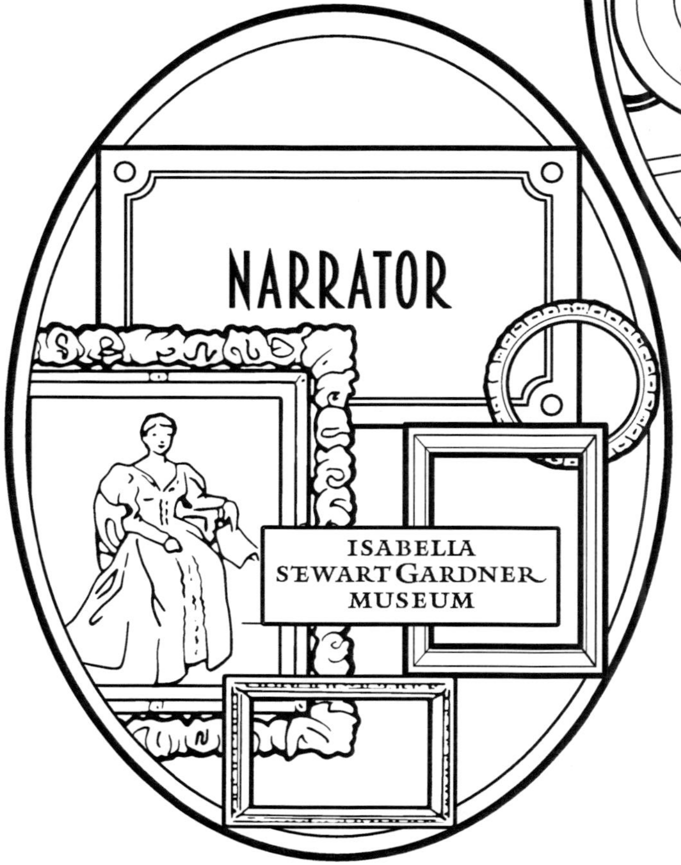

The Stolen Art Badge Art (cont.)

The Stolen Art Script

Setting

Act 1 takes place at the Isabella Stewart Gardner Museum in Boston. It is March 18, 1990. Act 2 takes place in the same location 25 years later.

Act 1

Narrator: Isabella Stewart Gardner was an art collector. She opened a museum in Boston in 1903. It was home to many famous paintings. They were stored safely in her museum. That is, until one fateful morning. It was March 18, 1990. Two security guards arrived for their work shift. But the night guards did not let them in. The museum was locked. The security guards were confused. So they called the police for help.

Officer Jones: [*knocking*] Open up! It's the Boston police.

Officer Wright: Something isn't right here. Where are the guards from last night?

Narrator: Anne Hawley arrived at the museum. She had a set of keys to unlock the doors. Anne was the museum director. She was in charge of the whole museum.

Anne: Hello, officers. My morning security guards called me. They said there was a problem. I came to make sure everything was okay.

Officer Jones: Good morning, Ms. Hawley. It looks like your guards from last night are gone.

Anne: Oh, my! Let me unlock the doors. Let's see what is going on.

Narrator: Anne unlocked the doors and they went inside. The museum was quiet. The night guards were supposed to be at the watch desk. But they were gone.

Randy and Rick: [*muffled*] Help! Help!

Officer Wright: Did you hear that? It's coming from downstairs.

Characters

- Narrator
- Security Guard Rick Abath
- Security Guard Randy Hestand
- Museum Director Anne Hawley
- Police Officer Jones
- Police Officer Wright

The Stolen Art Script *(cont.)*

Anne: It sounds like Randy and Rick. They are the missing guards. They must be trapped in the basement! Let's hurry.

Narrator: They found the two night guards in the basement. They were handcuffed to a bench.

Officer Jones: Let me unlock your handcuffs. Are you two all right?

Randy: I'm a little hungry. I missed my dinner break.

Rick: Yeah, me too. What a night. What time is it?

Officer Wright: It's 8:15 a.m. How long have you been down here?

Randy: Since about 2:00 in the morning.

Anne: Well, you both look unharmed. What in the world happened last night?

Randy: It started like any other night shift. Well, I can't exactly say that. It was my first time working as a night guard.

Rick: Randy sat at the watch desk. I did the first patrol. I had my walkie talkie and my flashlight. I made the rounds through the museum. It was just like any other night. The only difference was the commotion outside. There were crowds of people on the street.

Officer Wright: Why was there a crowd on the street so late at night?

Randy: It was St. Patrick's Day! There were parties everywhere. I was bummed that I had to work.

Officer Jones: Okay, so there were people outside. Then what happened? Did they come inside? How did you get handcuffed in the basement?

Rick: Whoa, slow down. I haven't gotten that far yet. Like I was saying, I was making the rounds. I did everything like I always do. I even opened and closed the side door.

Officer Wright: What do you mean? Why did you open and close the side door? Did you let someone in?

The Stolen Art Script *(cont.)*

Rick: No. I just like to check that the door is really locked. It was.

Anne: So you didn't notice anything unusual?

Randy: Rick, you forgot to tell them about the smoke alarms.

Anne: The building was on fire?

Rick: Ha! At first, I thought it was too. The fire alarms went off. I checked each room. But there was no fire. There was no hint of smoke. So I went into the security room and turned off the alarms.

Officer Jones: You turned off all the alarms? Why?

Rick: I thought the control panel was broken or something. I didn't want to hear fire alarms all night.

Officer Wright: [*groans*] Fair enough. What happened next?

Randy: Oh, this is my part! So next, the cops show up. They knocked on the door and said they needed to ask me some questions.

Officer Jones: The police? Why?

Randy: They said they were looking for Rick.

Anne: Rick, are you in some sort of trouble?

Rick: No, Ms. Hawley. At first, I thought they were responding to the fire alarms going off. But now that I think about it, it was just part of their plan.

Anne: Whose plan? The police?

Randy: I don't think they were really police.

Officer Wright: Why do you think they weren't the police?

Randy: Well, they said, "Gentlemen, this is a robbery!" Then they handcuffed us.

Rick: They took us to the basement and locked us in there.

The Stolen Art Script *(cont.)*

Randy: They came down to check on us. They asked if we were comfortable. That was nice. Oh, and they looked at our wallets. They said they knew where we lived. They said we would get a reward in one year.

Office Wright: So the fake police locked you in the basement? A reward for what? Did they steal anything?

Anne: [*gasps*] Let's find out.

Narrator: The museum has three floors full of artwork. There are thousands of paintings, sculptures, and books. Isabella was a big collector. Her gallery included very famous work. She had paintings by Matisse, Michelangelo, and Rembrandt. Anne, Randy, and Rick led the two officers through the museum. They stopped in every room.

Office Wright: Oh no. It looks like they did commit a robbery.

Narrator: They found frames torn off the wall. The glass was shattered on the floor. The paintings had been cut out of the frames.

Anne: [*crying*] No! Not the Degas! They took the Vermeer! Oh, no! They got the Rembrandt! That painting was my favorite!

Officer Jones: Don't worry, Ms. Hawley. We will find the thieves. We will get the paintings back.

Anne: They stole 13 paintings! That is close to $200 million dollars in artwork… gone.

Officer Wright: Two hundred million dollars!? For 13 paintings?

Anne: These are priceless works of art. They are not replaceable. I can't believe this has happened.

Officer Jones: We can solve this. Where do you keep the security cameras? Can we view the tapes of what happened in each part of the museum?

Anne: We only have cameras pointed at the front door, parking lot, and front desk. But we have motion detectors in all the rooms. It's all in the security office. I'll show you there.

The Stolen Art Script *(cont.)*

Narrator: When they entered the office, they could tell the thieves had been there.

Anne: Oh no! They took the videotapes. But we still have the motion detector recordings.

Narrator: When reviewing the motion detector alerts, they noticed something strange.

Officer Wright: The motion detector shows alerts to all the rooms the thieves stole artwork from except one.

Anne: You're right! The small Manet painting was stolen from the first floor gallery. Why did the motion detector not catch that?

Officer Jones: According to the data, Rick was the last person in that room.

Rick: Yes, when it was my turn to walk the museum floor. Wait, you think I stole it?

Anne: No, Rick. I know you wouldn't steal it. Plus, it was also cut from the frame. Why would they do that? It is small enough to carry with one hand.

Officer Wright: This case is a mystery. Why would anyone steal these paintings? They know they will get caught if they try to sell them.

Anne: Not only that. Why did they take the 13 that they did? My gallery has artwork worth more than some of the ones they took. It seems random.

Officer Jones: Actually, it doesn't seem random. It looks like they had a list of what they wanted and went for it.

Officer Wright: Most art thieves try to get in and out as fast as possible. These robbers were here for 81 minutes! They took their time.

Anne: I wish we had money for better security. This is a nightmare. Officers, is it okay if I send Rick and Randy home? They must be exhausted.

Officer Jones: Of course. Gentlemen, we will reach out if we have any more questions.

Randy: Thank you, Ms. Hawley. I'm very tired.

The Stolen Art Script *(cont.)*

The Stolen Art

Rick: Me too. Let us know if we can help with anything. I am really sorry this happened. I hope those thieves are caught!

Act 2

Narrator: Twenty-five years passed. The artwork was still missing. Officer Jones and Officer Wright returned to the museum. They wanted to talk with Anne some more.

Anne: Welcome back, officers. Still no new leads?

Officer Jones: We came back to tell you that the FBI released the names of the men they think stole the art.

Officer Wright: They were robbers who were working for someone else. Some people think they wanted to use the stolen art as a "get out of jail free" card. Or, maybe their crime boss was in jail at the time. They could use the art as a way to bargain for their boss to have a lower prison sentence.

Officer Jones: But they never had a chance to use the art that way. Both thieves died the year of the robbery.

Anne: Oh, my goodness! So where did they hide the art?

Officer Wright: That is still a mystery.

Officer Jones: Not one person has information on any of the 13 paintings.

Anne: We left all the empty frames on the wall. Isabella Gardner had a special request in her will. Her gallery was not to be changed in any way. I did my best to respect her wishes. I hope one day those empty frames are complete again.

Narrator: The mystery remains unsolved. There is a $10 million dollar reward to anyone who can help return the stolen art. What do *you* think happened?

The Stolen Art Activity

1. List one thing that was strange about the way the robbers stole the art.

____

____

2. What do you think Officer Wright meant when he said a thief might want to use the art as a "get out of jail free" card?

____

____

3. Why did Anne leave the empty frames hanging in the museum?

____

____

4. Do you think the art will ever be found? Why or why not?

____

____

____

Reader's Theater Reflections

Think about your performance. Color in the number of stars to show how well you did in each area.

Accuracy: I read my part correctly.	☆ ☆ ☆
Rate: I read at a pace that was not too fast or too slow.	☆ ☆ ☆
Expression: I read my character's part with feeling and emotion.	☆ ☆ ☆

List one way that you can improve your reader's theater performance.

____

____

The Stolen Art Journal

The FBI thinks they found the robbers. But they never found the stolen art. This case remains an unsolved mystery. Where do you think the missing artwork is today? Explain your thoughts.

The Stolen Art